TODAY'S SUPERPOWER:
BUILDING NETWORKS

TODAY'S SUPERPOWER: BUILDING NETWORKS

SEVEN MINDSETS PRINCIPLES TO THRIVE IN A FAST-CHANGING WORLD

MIKEL MANGOLD

NEW DEGREE PRESS

COPYRIGHT © 2022 MIKEL MANGOLD

All rights reserved.

TODAY'S SUPERPOWER: BUILDING NETWORKS

Seven Mindsets Principles to Thrive in a Fast-Changing World

ISBN   979-8-88504-127-0   *Paperback*

             979-8-88504-757-9   *Kindle Ebook*

             979-8-88504-236-9   *Ebook*

I dedicate this book to my parents, who always supported me in doing the things I am passionate about and never put pressure on me to get titles. To my brother Yannick and sister Léa-Marie Mangold.

Table of Contents

Introduction

Carl Djerassi (1923–2015) changed the world with his break-through invention of the contraceptive pill. He grew up in a middle-class family in Austria but had to flee his homeland to escape Nazi outrage and ended up in Bulgaria. He learned English and immigrated to the USA with his family shortly after. At the very young age of sixteen, he started his undergraduate studies majoring in chemistry. This man dedicated years of work to academia and the industry. He decided to move to Mexico, where he could scale his innovative ideas through collaboration and team efforts.

Carl could change the world by starting his career in one specific field: chemistry. And he succeeded. However, let's consider that Carl grew up in a time when companies were working in a vertical structure, meaning niche markets or products, e.g., chemicals, manufacturing, or construction. Career advice of that time was to focus on one specific topic. He couldn't. Due to the war, he was forced to move countries and followed the best academic or industrial job openings. His problems turned to become opportunities. This mix of experience—a network of disciplines—made him go faster than his peers. Later, Carl discovered and promoted the importance of interdisciplinary networks.

I learned valuable insights about Carl from his interview with Roger Kornberg, editor of the *Annual Review of Biochemistry* and professor at the department of structural biology at the Stanford University School of Medicine, particularly about the importance of collaboration (Annual Reviews, 2012):

"If I started my career again, I would not become a chemistry major. Pure chemistry is the discipline, but the fascinating part of chemistry is the connection to physics, material science, and biology; it's the collaboration between them…the actual driving force."

Carl incorporated the knowledge he gained from past experiences into new projects, pushed boundaries, and broke down silos. His highly inquisitive nature led him to different fields such as history and art. He even became a fiction writer and a poet, and at the end of his life, he possessed a gigantic art collection. His relentless curiosity and open mindset to explore new fields was the main reason behind his ability to build novel transformative pharmaceuticals and agricultural products.

Have you ever wondered what solves the problems of our world and what influences how we live our daily lives? Through the birth control pill he developed, Carl empowered women by allowing them to choose when to become pregnant.

What enables people like Carl to change society? What made it possible for Steve Jobs to bring the iPhone and the Apple Store to people's hands? Networks.

Why is it even more relevant today? You and I are witnessing the most significant change our civilization has ever faced. I have realized something particularly new to us, brought on by the new knowledge economy and the digitalization of everything: the availability of networks. In today's world, it's never been so easy to have access to them. I believe these networks can and should be used to create positive societal changes. More on what I mean by networks a little bit later in Chapter 2.

Over the last decade, I have noticed something interesting. Most of today's innovations, products, and services combine several disciplines. Cars are now computers, medical hardware are directly connected to the cloud and uses predictive algorithms for improved care, materials are made with nanotechnologies to enhance their properties such as conductivity and transparency, and so on. Hence, nobody can create a significant change in today's world without being connected to someone or something that provides the missing part for their big idea.

THE NEED FOR A CROSS-SILO APPROACH

People like Carl Djerassi show us that implementing a significant change—like introducing the birth control pill to society—comes from a combination of ideas collected from different environments with different people, institutions, or organizations. One of my inspirations to write this book was to investigate if Carl's experience was unique or something future change-makers could learn from.

As humans, we prefer comfort zones rather than dealing with the unknown. Most people worry about changing and pursuing new learning paths. However, we shouldn't avoid it.

Have you heard about the acronym VUCA? Yes, **V**olatility, **U**ncertainty, **C**omplexity, and **A**mbiguity. This acronym became popular in the early 1980s to spread awareness about our world. Whether we like it or not, it's a new reality. Not accepting uncertainty and working in silos—only on one business vertical—is an issue. I will try to convince anyone reading this book—with data and insights—that moving outside your silos is necessary to thrive, succeed, and change the world.

Of chemists, for example, Carl says (Annual Reviews, 2012):

"The mode of operation of chemists dehumanizes you...In my department that contained more than twenty people, less than three people have read the books I read, have been to the places I have been to, and have been to the theaters I have been to. That cultural curiosity does not exist in the chemist community—most of them have little cultural intellectual curiosity... half of the Stanford chemist's students have never been to a theater. I am very unhappy about this."

I can genuinely empathize with Carl here. As a chemist by training, I saw with my own eyes how the vast majority of my colleagues kept their interests restricted during their entire academic life. As a result, very few of them use their incredible knowledge to change the way we live and work. None of my chemist friends ended up being entrepreneurs. At least, until now. Many stopped being ambitious and tried to secure a safe job. I think this is sad because we lose educated people who would have been capable of leading a significant positive change like the one Carl led.

Most importantly, the current corporate model inspired by the industrial revolution is starting to fade. The weaknesses of this model can be seen in the statistics featured below.

THE PROBLEMS OUR SOCIETY FACES

Today, we live in an age of exponential technologies that drive our world forward—to name a few, artificial intelligence, the internet of things, 3D printing, blockchain, cloud computing. These digital technologies use network effects that can scale much faster than what we've previously experienced in the industrial world (Bonchek, 2016). As Peter Diamandis mentions, we will experience more change in this decade—2020 to 2030—than in the past one hundred years (Corbyn, 2020). On top of that, unpredictability is a new reality. McKinsey & Company investigated the latest trends in the article "The Next Normal Arrives Trends That Will Define 2021—and Beyond." The article explores recent findings related to the COVID-19 pandemic and its effects: forcing people to work from home, boosting digital transformation, and changing consumer behavior in the long run. Furthermore, an increasing number of startups are being created, and more and more people are deciding to launch their businesses (Sneader and Singhal, 2021)

People within organizations are losing engagement and leaving their jobs, and in the worst-case scenario, getting fired. The gig economy is on the rise. A big wave of employees also experiences a lack of trust and belonging in their professional lives. Finally, the young generation feels hopeless about their future. The message is clear: There is a decline in corporate innovation, and corporations and individuals are no longer happy with the old model.

The following data points show our society faces a real crisis:

- According to Innosight's 2016 report "Corporate Longevity: Turbulence Ahead for Large Organizations," corporations in the S&P 500 Index in 1965 stayed there for thirty-three years on average. By 1990, the same index presented a reduction in the average tenure to twenty years. The future is even more revealing, with a forecast of only fourteen years by 2026 (Anthony, Viguerie, and Waldeck, 2016).
- Only 13 percent of employees are passionate and engaged at work (Hagel et al., 2017)
- An O.C. Tanner Learning Group study investigated over 200,000 people across ten years and revealed that 65 percent of employees reported a lack of recognition, and 79 percent of people who quit their jobs cite "lack of appreciation" as their reason for leaving.
- During the COVID-19 pandemic, a study in the UK surveyed 2,000 people aged sixteen to twenty-five, showing more than half (57 percent) of young people is "scared" about being unemployed and 43 percent are worried they will never be able to get a job (Harding, 2020).

- The COVID-19 crisis also pushed millions of workers to quit their job. This trend, called "The Great Resignation," is mainly noticeable in the US and globally (Tharoor, 2021).

If our society continues heading in this direction, it may experience a shattering crisis. Just like in any other macroeconomic shock, the impact can be immense: billions of people will be affected and suffer from it, wealth disparity will increase, inflation and exponential growth in unemployment rates, not to mention the direct impact on the stability of governments and peace. At the same time, society's biggest problems—such as climate change and our political order—will remain or even get worse.

We must change.

I am a millennial, and one thing for sure is my generation does not want to just work for money. We are looking for meaning and purpose. From the thousands of discussions I've had with the people I have met, I have noticed the strong desire of many individuals to change society for the better, but they feel stuck and don't have any idea how to become a change agent. They don't know where to start or how to scale an idea. For instance, my friend Duy, whom I met at TEDx San Francisco as a volunteer, mentioned he would love to help his home country Vietnam to better prepare for and alleviate the consequences of climate change. He believes climate action requires collective efforts from networks of people so change can happen sustainably. During our conversations, he said he would love to be part of the solution and serve his country, but unfortunately, he doesn't know the starting point: *How* does one create and become the change?

I was motivated to write this book upon considering the complex problems our world faces today: COVID-19, political instability, corruption, deforestation, the extensive use of natural resources, the supply chain crisis, the double-digit decline of wildlife populations over just a few decades, inequitable access to education, the lack of inclusion, unemployment, poverty, and many other issues. Globally, a third of people globally don't have access to safe drinking water. That's one in three people—representing 2.2 billion people around the world. As if that's not bad enough, "4.2 billion people do not have safely managed sanitation services, and three billion lack basic handwashing facilities" (WHO, 2019).

Do you believe all these problems can be solved if only 13 percent of the workforce is engaged? The answer is crystal clear: It is impossible! We need more change-makers, more people who will dedicate their lives to solve problems. Using networks in today's digital era is the opportunity.

WHAT IS MY STORY? WHY THIS BOOK?

As I mentioned earlier, I am a chemist by training. This also explains why I started this book with Carl Djerassi. I studied six and a half years of pure chemistry with a minor in cultural studies and communication. In addition to the four and half years I studied in Freiburg, Germany, I also studied for a year in France, eight months in Switzerland, and four months in Mexico. I realized that studying pure chemistry doesn't make me an innovator, nor someone who can change society purely through business. My peers and I became well-disciplined scientists who knew where to research and how to present data. However, in general, scientists like to stay in their fields of expertise and avoid the macro-level analysis of a problem.

Companies around the world are spending millions of dollars on their innovation programs, looking for innovators and change-makers. However, merely spending energy and money is not an effective strategy for innovation. The real change drivers are the individuals who both have the right mindset and are plugged into the best networks.

Let me repeat that: It is so much more about mindset, people, and networks.

Skills and knowledge in isolation do not always bring the change you need. Discipline, conscientiousness, and ceaseless research are no longer enough. You need more. You need to connect with people and drive collaboration. You need access to insights and create a feedback loop—collecting fast and frequent feedback from your customers and stakeholders to increase your chances of adapting to emerging changes.

Alexander Osterwalder and colleagues further support my position in their *Harvard Business Review* article *"Why Your Organization Needs an Innovation Ecosystem"*:

"Of course, even with the best in-house talent and innovation process, companies cannot come up with the best ideas on their own. That's why a complete innovation ecosystem requires collaboration with external innovators. Just look at successful

tech companies Tencent and Alibaba: according to the Financial Times, they generate over a third of their revenues from investments in external startups."

I am fortunate to have traveled to thirty-six countries while still in my twenties, including eight countries in Africa. Through my trips I met thousands of people from different cultures, ethnicities, and mindsets. You cannot imagine how much these experiences opened my eyes and mind. I also had the privilege to work in San Francisco and Silicon Valley in 2019 and 2020, just before the COVID-19 pandemic started. In Chapter 3, I will share what I experienced and the key lessons I learned there. Here is a teaser: entrepreneurs in Silicon Valley never succeed by themselves; they succeed as a network of people! It's about the people, working with an open mind in a thriving ecosystem.

In this book, I will present seven mindset principles that will give you the power to collaborate, enabling you to improve your ideas, to find resources such as capital or intellectual property, and to attract talented people to join your mission. I will share my own experiences to explain why networks matter.

For example, when I was in Silicon Valley, I had the opportunity to meet a brilliant investor and serial founder. Out of respect for her privacy, I'm just going to call her Josepha. I learned a fundamental truth from her. Outstanding businesses are not successful because of their products or services. A business can only grow, thrive, and create meaningful change if the people working for that organization feel part of the mission and want to devote their time and energy to the future of the company.

In one of our calls, Josepha told me a story from her early twenties. The company owner—her manager—sent her to Canada, where a company was floundering. He told her, "The company is failing, and employees are leaving. Take my credit card, find out what the problem is, and fix it." She went there, conducted one-on-one interviews with nearly all the employees, and two key issues emerged:

1. The management team didn't fit together; the relationship between them wasn't good.
2. Nearby companies—the competition—were treating their employees better with higher salaries and better conditions. As a result, many employees started to leave the company to join the competition.

She instituted new directives regarding the decision-making process of the company and increased the salary of almost everyone. The employee retention finally improved, and a few years later, the owner (who gave her his credit card years before) sold this successful company and made millions in profit.

Talented people, business planning, or strategy are completely useless if you can't make people work together and collaborate. People stay if they feel supported and empowered. Building a network of trust among the people is the future.

It is about caring. A specific mindset is required to tackle problems and turn them into opportunities. Is this mindset problem the same everywhere? No.

UNITED STATES VS. EUROPE MINDSET: DO PEOPLE BEHAVE DIFFERENTLY?

At the time of writing this book, I also worked as an Innovation Project Manager in Germany. In my interactions with many European stakeholders, I noticed how vastly different the European way of work was from that of Silicon Valley.

My observation was supported by the 2021 McKinsey & Company article "Building the European Biotech Sector with World-Class Science and Innovation." It talks about the strengths and weaknesses of Europe:

"Europe is a powerhouse in scientific publishing with roughly twice the output of the United States and three times that of China...Despite Europe's strength in science and innovation, translation remains the biggest challenge. Translation of science into companies is stagnant. The distribution of newly funded biotechs remains unchanged across geographies over the last six years, and Europe accounts for only 25 percent of new biotechs. Future success will depend on improving the translation of research into new companies, raising more capital, and building entrepreneurial talent."

Scientific papers or intellectual property alone don't change society much. What really matters is that ideas get converted and put in people's hands. In that sense, Europe is lagging. We need more people embracing the values of entrepreneurship such as taking risks and thinking long term. A joint effort has to be made between governments, founders, and investors to keep Europe at the edge of innovation & technology.

As part of his work on the thesis of his MBA in Digital Transformation, Florenz Unold asked the following question in a survey: "How would you rate the importance of the following potential building blocks of corporate Idea & Innovation Management (I2M)?" Seventy-eight corporate innovators participated in the study. The outcome is telling.

People and Skills ranked as the most important building block of Idea and Innovation Management, at 65 percent. This is followed by *Innovation Network* (41 percent), *Organizational Structure* (40 percent), and *Innovation Portfolio* (37 percent). This clearly shows mindset, people skills, and networks are the most important elements in the innovation process—not tools or processes.

This tells us that creating change and innovation is about the combination of tools, mindset, and networks. While most people have the tools to succeed (i.e., education, processes), many lack the mindset and the network to create a meaningful change in society. In this book, I am putting the focus on mindset and networks.

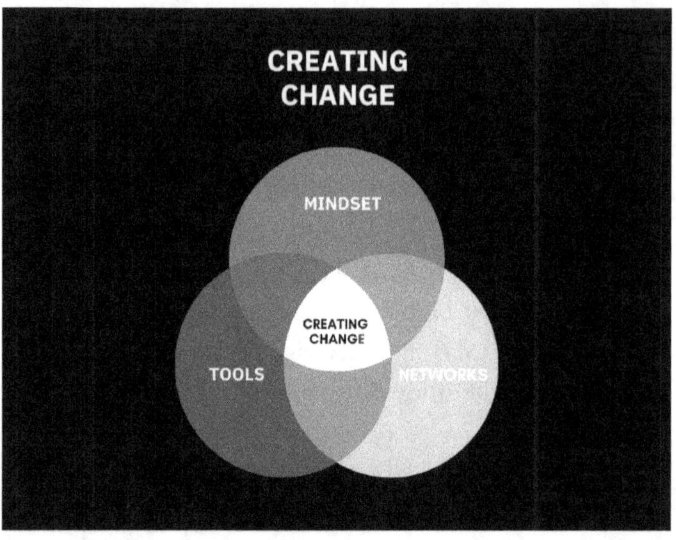

Why is there such a huge difference between Europe and the US, and specifically Silicon Valley, when it comes to entrepreneurial talent and the conversion of knowledge into innovation? Kim Baroudy and colleagues (2020) help us to understand it a bit better:

1. Entrepreneurs are less celebrated in Europe than in the US: "About 17 percent of press coverage in Germany portrays entrepreneurship in a positive light, as compared with 39 percent in the United States."

2. In Europe, there is a lower concentration of entrepreneurs: "Innovation 'superhubs' are not as densely packed with resources as those in the United States. Only about 30 percent of European startups have located their headquarters in a tech superhub (Berlin, London, Paris, Stockholm)—versus almost half of US startups." The result is lower interaction and, consequently, less serendipity.

Today, major societal change is triggered by entrepreneurs or people with an entrepreneurial mindset. Obviously, they are not alone in doing this, but they are the primary driving force. This book is NOT about how to do some business networking or which tool to use to innovate and develop a product. This book focuses on the mindset individuals have to adopt to thrive and create positive change in today's startup and multistakeholder economy, collaboration being the essence of it.

WHAT IS THIS BOOK ABOUT AND WHAT TO EXPECT

Even though change seems challenging and hard, there is always a way out. For example, if you need to fix a water pipe at home, you can go to YouTube to see how to do it, and you can send a message to that person and ask for additional advice. Beyond that, you can even post a poll online where scores of people can vote and make recommendations to you about what to buy. In a matter of a few hours, you solved your problem through the power of networks. I believe networks are the solution to solving both small problems as well as the world's biggest problems like climate change or giving everyone access to education. Similarly, networks will also help you advance way faster than you imagine in your life and career.

Most people think of the term "network" as "networking," i.e., the practice of meeting people at a conference or shaking hands in business meetings. For me, networks are much more than that. This book is going to talk about three types of networks: (1) knowledge, (2) resources, and (3) people.

In Chapter 1, we will look at a short overview of the history of innovation. This is followed by a deep dive into networks and why they are so effective, in Chapter 2. Chapter 3 is about Silicon Valley and six things it is doing right. From there, I will introduce to you seven mindset principles. You will learn how to create, join, or leverage the power of networks. Finally, we conclude the book with a look into the future.

The seven mindset principles are aimed at helping anyone to gain the superpower of our time: building networks. People who have a strong ability to build networks will have better ideas than those who don't. They have greater access to resources such as capital, databases, infrastructures, and they have a competitive advantage by attracting talented people to their work. Understanding your strengths and weaknesses related to these principles will not only allow you to determine your individual capability to influence change but can also be used as a blueprint for increasing it over time.

Mindset Principle 1—DO-IT-YOURSELF, Take Ownership: Take initiatives, be entrepreneurial, and tell good stories to invite others to join your mission.

Mindset Principle 2—Blow Up Borders: Move outside your silos, go toward the unknown, learn from it, and come back. Embrace diversity and welcome new perspectives.

Mindset Principle 3—Be of Value. Give Before You Get: Remove your ego and stop your desire to always receive something in return. When you help others, it always comes back to you stronger.

Mindset Principle 4—Start Small, Grow Big, with Purpose: Identifying a shared purpose will attract people to you. Be transparent and share ideas.

Mindset Principle 5—Do What You Can't: It's about pursing a project despite everybody telling you it can't be done. By doing so, the people being inspired will support and join your mission.

Mindset Principle 6—Go Viral: Use the incredibly powerful tool of our time: social media. Build trust and bond with people without spending too much time.

Mindset Principle 7—Be Bold and Have Skin in the Game: Take the majority of the risks; be courageous and bold. As a direct consequence, you create credibility, reliability, and accountability.

A friend of mine asked me to define "change." He asked, "How big is the change you are talking about?" In this book, I will be talking about both small changes and big changes, because I believe major changes are the consequences of many minor changes. Networks can be used to write a book and share a message to thousands of people or to build the next billion-dollar company impacting billions of lives.

In this book, we will talk about innovation (ideas delivered into consumers hands via a business), not only from startups, but also from major multinational companies. We will talk about ecosystems and the art of building successful businesses through networks. I interviewed and collected advice from over twenty successful innovators and businesspeople from around the world—consultants, founders, and CEOs of billion-dollar funds. Moreover, I added world-changing stories found on the web. Last but not least, every chapter will be filled with data and personal anecdotes.

WHO IS THIS BOOK FOR?

The people who create change in society, like Carl Djerassi, know it is all about interdisciplinarity networks. The best networks focus on generosity and collaboration. The people involved with these networks prioritize action over thinking and are very curious individuals. They move outside of their silos to get multi-disciplinary exposure. They learn from others. By doing so, they are capable of identifying a shared mission, goal, and values, which helps scale a transformative idea.

This is a book for *wantrepreneurs*—someone who would like to start a business and thinks and talks about doing so, but never gets started (Macmillan, 2021)—and aspiring change-makers, especially the ones located outside of innovation hubs like Silicon Valley, Boston, Israel, London, or Shenzhen. Additionally, it is for all the people involved in the innovation industry, working with startups and with their ecosystem to build successful companies.

In today's digital era and current corporate landscape, it is a reality that anyone—including you—are capable of reshaping society for the better. Focusing on a single business vertical in this day and age will make us vulnerable and unadaptable. Collaboration has never been so important as now. Trust is the glue. This book should give you the confidence to start your big idea by creating, joining, and leveraging the power of networks.

Let's roll with Chapter 1 and learn more about the history of innovation.

PART 1

THE IMPORTANCE OF NETWORKS FOR INNOVATION

CHAPTER 1

History of Innovation and Change-Making

———

"The industrial revolution turned the timetable and the assembly line into a template for almost all human activities."

—*YUVAL NOAH HARARI*

We all follow the cultural norms of our society, but we often don't think about the rationale behind their existence. Are they helping us? Or do they make us worse?

Timetables, rules, and processes structure our days and work life and are part of the culture of most organizations. Today, we follow most of the rules unconsciously, and the reality is that all these corporate rules are human made and didn't exist a few centuries ago. Time monitoring pushed workers to work long hours and increased output in the Industrial Revolution (Chong, 2020). It has worked well in enhancing productivity at production lines and has enabled substantial economic growth for developing countries.

Timetables are just one of the rules people have followed and respected. In the twentieth century, it became the "new normal" and over time, many have tried to trademark and officialize other processes such as Six Sigma℠, ISO 9000®, Stage Gate®, Taleo® (a system to hire people), and more.

There were reasons behind this. The rise of the industrial revolution saw the production of a massive amount of goods, and after the second world war, the world had to be rebuilt, again leading to an increase in production. As a result, regulations, and processes were created and implemented. They have helped people and organizations replicate the success with high quality and efficiency and automate decisions. Additionally, poverty—not inequality—was much bigger back then. Many wanted to work in factories to get money. In this old way of doing things, the focus was on productivity, counting hours, taking decisions to benefit people and companies right away—not long term—and revenues were presented quarterly to please shareholders. In the old world, this model *was* successful.

Nevertheless, we have evolved. Today, we have new problems, and solving them requires a different approach.

Our world's biggest problems (pandemics, the scarcity of water, food waste, malnutrition, inequality, world peace) won't be solved by governments, corporations, or billionaires. Those larger systemic changes will be made by partnerships with a long-term outlook. When individuals, consumers, suppliers, and corporates collaborate, and the right partnerships are made, the positive change cannot only be more significant, but also drastically accelerated. Due to the urgency of our time, those partnerships are not nice to have; they are must-haves. Hence, our new economy is long-term, using a multistakeholder business model. It's ecosystem driven, full of startups, with people working in networks. Innovation and knowledge are at the core of the new model, and here the flat structure is standard, enabling information to flow faster through the different stakeholders.

Companies and individuals will need to develop deep connections with employees, communities, business partners, governments, civil organizations and more to make it work. This new economy is about creating a trusted ecosystem where people value honesty and accountability. When you work and behave that way, you solve more problems and the impact on the world is significantly more. Indeed, you not only change the world positively, but you also generate wealth and become more successful.

Paul Polman is the former CEO of Unilever, and Andrew Winston is a globally recognized expert on megatrends and how to build companies that thrive by serving the world. They co-authored the book, *Net Positive: How Courageous Companies Thrive by Giving More Than They Take*, wherein they talk about how Unilever was ahead of its competitors during the world-changing COVID-19 crisis in 2020. "Unilever, moved faster than its peers because of the trust it has built up with stakeholders over the years."

If Unilever—one of the biggest companies in the world—could embrace this new model. Why not you?

BE A PART OF THE CHANGE

The problem is too many people inside organizations and in our society overall are emotionally dead. Ninety-six percent of people in the UK admit to making most decisions on autopilot mode (Razzetti, 2018). They do not even realize they can be a part of the change! Most individuals are afraid to challenge the status quo. They prefer to keep what they have instead of creating a new tomorrow. They are fearful and follow the rules without asking themselves the most important question—why?

We need more change-makers in every company and organization. Typically, those individuals have an entrepreneurial approach to life, are focused on solving problems, and have a specific mindset and behavioral traits. These people thrive in the new economy. The experience gained from creating change and fixing problems makes you future-ready; you will be better able to handle uncertainty and discomfort.

The truth is, being that person and trying to create change is demanding and requires a lot of energy and grit. Many will not understand this, and to be honest with you, we know shutting your mouth and following rules is more manageable than calling out for a change and taking steps to make it happen.

Early in 2021, I posted a cartoon on LinkedIn, curious to see what people thought about it. On the first panel of the comic, a man is speaking to a crowd, asking, "Who wants to change?" and everyone in the group has their hands raised, smiling eagerly. In the next panel, the speaker asks, "Who wants to change?" and no hands are raised; everyone looks dejected. In the final panel, the speaker asks, "Who wants to lead the change?" and the crowd is gone. My caption was, "Be the leader of the change; who is joining me in the third box?" The post received over 40,000 views, and more than eighty-five comments confirmed this sad reality: Nobody wants to lead the change.

One person in particular, Jonathan Reynolds, California-based CEO of Mindful Life, Mindful Work, commented the following:

"Great cartoon!

Ultimately there is no choice, as change is going to happen whether we want it to or not...It is, after all, the very fabric of reality. If we commit to change, we infuse a given system with real and exciting possibility; if we avoid the reality of change, all we get is degeneration and the inevitable decay of entropy.

Embracing and cultivating change and growth is so very empowering, and to do otherwise is to situate ourselves as a victim of change, as an object without autonomy and volition. There is a word for things that don't change and grow vibrantly and dynamically; the word is 'dead'...dead physically, psychologically, systemically, and otherwise.

Change is not easy, but it is essential to be truly alive as individuals and organizations. To cling to the familiar and 'the calcified' is undoubtedly the death of any endeavor.

And remember, it's the first adopter that joins the leader that plays the most crucial role in getting buy-in from the rest!"

To be alive as an individual or as a business, we have to grow and progress. Creating positive change is a great way to feel fulfilled and feel a sense of purpose.

A good representation of people implementing change is entrepreneurs. For me, it is a perfect use case. It is always about introducing a new idea to the market by creating value and removing a problem. At first, many people reject it, then you get some early adopters, and finally, if successful, the masses will adopt it. Overall, this process is arduous and full of obstacles. Our society needs more entrepreneurs and entrepreneurial minds. The truth is, being a part of a large organization doesn't always welcome this behavior, and many want to feel part of something bigger.

As a result, the startup culture is rising, and the new economy will mainly emerge from them. Let's explore how organizations innovated in the past, how it is changing, and how everyone has to adapt to the new world.

YESTERDAY'S INNOVATION CAME FROM R&D LABS; INNOVATION LABS AND STARTUPS WILL DRIVE TO-MORROW'S INNOVATION AND ECONOMY

Let's face it: Today's most significant digital innovation does not come from large corporations; it comes from startups. What has led to so many startups, and what is the relationship to today's digital, multistakeholder, and bottom-up economy?

According to Brad Feld in his book, *The Startup Community Way: Evolving an Entrepreneurial Ecosystem*, four significant events shaped the new economy:

1. The great depression of 1929 to 1933: Employees felt insecure and not part of their company anymore due to the crisis. Young people started to think about how else they could contribute to society. Opportunities evaporated from New York City, and many moved to California (today's Silicon Valley) to start businesses.
2. The emergence of key technologies: In the early 2000s, ubiquitous high-speed internet, smartphones, and cloud computing finally made starting a business from anywhere not only possible but also cheaper and more accessible.
3. The low-interest-rate strategy adopted by central banks worldwide: Persistently low interest rates pushed unprecedented amounts of financial capital into startups globally. Investors searched for riskier assets, such as venture capital, to generate higher returns. This continues today.
4. A broader set of actors pushed the entrepreneurial movement forward: President Obama announced, "Startup America," a national initiative designed to cultivate startup community development throughout the United

States. Many other venture capital funds followed, which focused on early-stage investment, as did the growing number of corporate venture capital groups. With that, a range of support mechanisms, like accelerators, incubators, and other models, snowballed in size and scope.

While these events happened in the US, the trend is growing in Europe as well. Take my home country, France, for example. President Macron vowed in 2018 to make France a "startup nation" (Alderman, 2018). The same trend is happening in Germany. The number of startups will double annually in the country until 2030. Startups will become the backbone of its economy generating over 1.4 million jobs and boosting economic growth (McKinsey & Company, 2021). This trend is not only a US, German, or French one. The movement is global.

According to a MIT and Capgemini study (Thompson, Bonnet, and Jaballah, 2020), innovation coming from the outside world is becoming increasingly relevant for companies:

"Over the next five years, startups will rank as top innovation sources for companies. Moreover, hybrid forms such as innovation labs are essential as an interface between internal and external innovation. It is even more relevant for companies that do not have to innovate internally. Many are forced to source externally. As a result of this development, traditional R&D and internal business units' employees will become less relevant as innovation sources within the next five years."

The study's authors surveyed over 320 global companies and asked them about their top three innovation sources;

internal (central R&D, Innovation Labs with dedicated and operational business staff) vs. external (suppliers, universities, third party, customers, startups, competitors, crowd). According to the respondents, 69 percent of innovation came from R&D, 33 percent from innovation labs, and only 10 percent from startups. The study's author prediction for 2025 looks significantly different:

- 29 percent from R&D
- 71 percent from innovation labs
- 44 percent from startups

Forward-thinking companies—the ones adapting to the change and aiming to solve the world's biggest problems with cutting-edge technologies—enhance collaboration with the outside world. The new model is ecosystem-driven—in other words, different players working together as networks. They embrace agile values and give more freedom to employees to test and implement their ideas.

One of the biggest pharmaceutical companies in the world realized it had to change. "Roche used to be so secretive...but now they are doing things they wouldn't have done before. There has been a wind of change" (Hollinger, Mancini, and Jack, 2020).

Why did Roche decide to change, and what has changed? Let's explore why there is no choice anymore.

TRANSFORMATIVE INNOVATION IS IMPERATIVE; THE NEW ECONOMY IS INTERDISCIPLINARY AND MORE LIKELY TO EMERGE FROM THRIVING ECOSYSTEMS

The reality is Roche and other companies have to change due to exponential technologies and disruptive innovation. Alone, they are too slow. A few decades are enough to bring those multinationals into obsolescence if they do not. So, what are exponential technologies? It is a technology that doubles in power or processing speed in every prescribed slice of time while its cost of ownership halves (IGI Global, 2021). In other words, technologies that can change millions more lives in a matter of hours, days, or months. Examples are quantum computing, big data, the internet of things (IoT), etc.

Clayton Christensen often named as the father of the term *disruptive innovation*, defined two types of invention in his famous 1995 *Harvard Business Review* article, "Disruptive Technologies: Catching the Wave" (Bower and Christensen, 1995):

- The first type of innovation, also called "business as usual," entails simply improving the existing systems, structures, and established ways of doing things. The organization's services, products, procedures, structures, and identity remain the same. This type of innovation is called *sustaining innovation* because it sustains business as usual.
- The second type of innovation described by Christensen is *disruptive innovation*. He identified a wide range of cases where competitors caught out companies. The competitors had invented entirely new services or products with a new business model that made the incumbent, or "business as usual" companies, completely irrelevant.

Common examples of disruptive innovation are Amazon, which disrupted the book-selling industry, and Netflix, which disrupted Blockbuster. It also exists in the scientific world: Genentech was also a disruptive company (now belonging to Roche). They disrupted the pharmaceutical landscape by introducing new biotechnology, e.g., cloning genetically engineered DNA in foreign cells and mass-producing the resulting drugs. (Leuty, 2016)

The kind of innovation that disrupts an industry is, according to the literature, called *transformative innovation.* (Terwilliger, 2015)

To survive in this dynamic world, companies have to make significant changes to how they are structured. One of the solutions to overcome this challenge is to work as a thriving ecosystem. This means working with multiple stakeholders as a network.

Pharma companies, for instance, are increasingly sourcing new molecular entities from startups because the variety of innovative strategies means more chances of success. (Geilinger and Leo, 2019). Related to the pharma industry, in March 2021, I co-published the academic paper, "What Corporates Can Do to Help an Innovation Ecosystem Thrive—and Why They Should Do It in the Journal of Commercial Biotechnology." I co-wrote the publication with Susan Windham-Bannister (the former CEO of the Massachusetts Live Sciences Center, a one-billion-dollar investment fund for biotech innovation) and Diana Joseph (founder of the Corporate Accelerator Forum in the San Francisco Bay Area). This paper provided a framework for how Boston successfully built its "innovation capacity" in the life sciences and became one of the most innovative places in the world in just twenty years.

In 2008, then-Governor Deval Patrick and the Massachusetts legislature created a ten-year, one-billion-dollar initiative to transform Massachusetts from a leading life sciences academic research hub to a world-leading life sciences innovation hub, where new technologies could be translated, developed, and commercialized. Today, Boston is recognized as the best life science ecosystem globally.

Patrick's team, including Susan Windham-Bannister, focused on building the long-term goal of innovation capacity: knowing how to produce one innovation after another on a sustained basis. In Windham-Bannister's framework, innovation capacity was built around five enablers.

1. Academic culture
2. Entrepreneurial culture (including risk capital)
3. Workforce
4. Infrastructure
5. The ecosystem

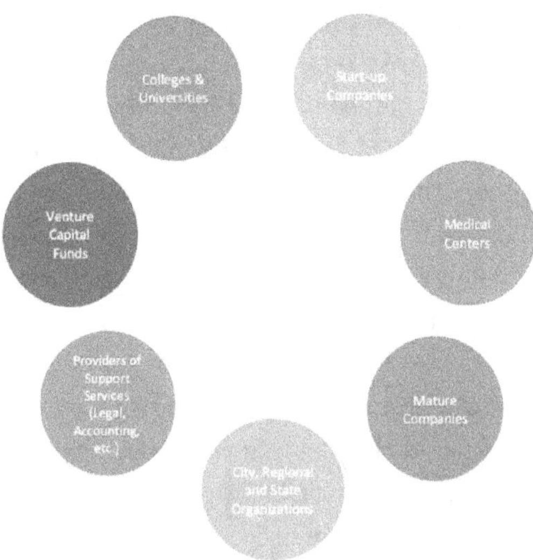

This is a cluster

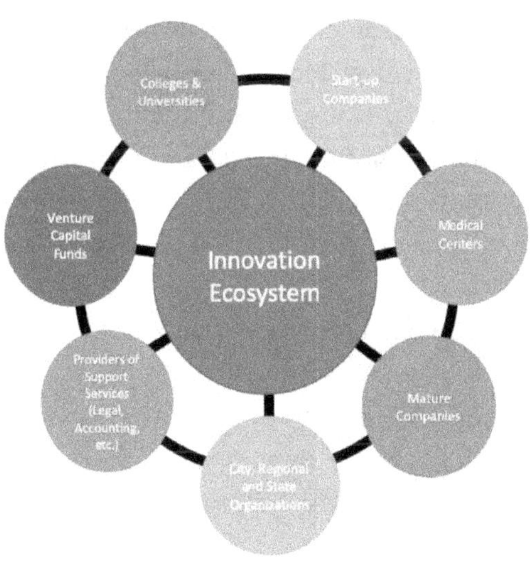

This is a thriving ecosystem

Boston succeeded because it utilized a backbone organization called Massachusetts Life Sciences Center (MSLC) to build a thriving ecosystem. The multi-layered nature of this network, which included investors, founders, scientists, and corporations, resulted in new pipelines for resource transfer throughout the network. They made diversity (different stakeholders and talents) and collaboration core principles. They also defined a clear purpose, a long-term shared view, and a structure to attract players.

Contrast this with universities. Most of them are, in fact, laggards. I studied chemistry at the University of Freiburg, Germany. As far as I could tell, the program we had to follow was almost the same they used to teach in the 1980s. The content had barely changed. At the beginning of my studies in 2011, the different chemistry departments were utterly isolated from each other. Organic chemistry, inorganic or mineral chemistry, macromolecular chemistry, biology, physical chemistry, and chemical biology were all separated. And not only did they not collaborate, but they were also in competition with one another. Instead of sharing resources to pursue research projects, they didn't communicate until a publication was published.

Why? Because it has always been that way.

The good news is, like Roche, the University of Freiburg realized it had to change. By 2018, just at the end of my master's degree studies, research departments started to have new profiles:

- Professor Esser joined the organic chemistry department in 2015, despite her research being on organic batteries (which is primarily macromolecular chemistry).
- Professor Anna Fischer joined the inorganic chemistry department in 2014, despite her focus on electrochemical energy conversion storage material, which is primarily a mixture of physics and macromolecular chemistry.
- Professor Walther joined the department of macromolecular chemistry in 2017, despite his focus on living organisms and bio-inspired materials.

They knew they had to make the research departments more interdisciplinary and enhance collaboration. Why? Because being close to other research departments and focusing on one specific expertise was more damaging to their research than being collaborative and interdisciplinary. They didn't have all the experts they needed to draw the correct conclusion from their experiences; they had to collaborate.

When different research departments or companies are interconnected, everyone wins. In my opinion, the resistance to mixing things up is due to the need for control and certainty. Today, we need to create an environment where ambiguity and uncertainty can stay under control and leverage experimentation. We need a cultural and, most importantly, mindset change.

In terms of culture, a great example is Silicon Valley. I experienced it myself in 2019 and 2020. The region has a bottom-up culture of openness, collaboration, and a commitment to the area over individual people, companies, and institutions.

They succeed as a network, not as individuals or corporate entities—more about this in Chapter 3.

All evidence points to the need to work together as an ecosystem and network. If we know this is the way to go, why are some companies resisting change?

BECOMING AN AGENT OF CHANGE AND INNOVATION

As a visionary businessman in the 1950s, Peter Drucker held a strong view about innovation and its importance to the corporate world. He had spread the message that companies that do not promote change would age and deteriorate and highlighted the decline is even faster in a period of high volatility. It is sad to realize most companies usually wait to be in a crisis or state of emergency to create change.

To surf the wave of change, companies need to have a leadership embracing and promoting innovation as well as employees acting as "innovation agents." Most of the time, people think money solves everything, but as the PwC report, "2018 Global Innovation 1000 Study" states, "dedicating more funds to innovation will not automatically generate growth." The report identifies six characteristics (referred to as the innovation DNA) the most innovative companies—Microsoft, Apple, Volkswagen, and Samsung—have in common:

1. Close alignment of innovation strategy with business strategy.
2. Company-wide cultural support of innovation.
3. Leadership is closely involved with the innovation program.

4. Base innovation on direct insights from end-users.
5. Rigorous control of project selection early in the innovation process.
6. Integrating the five characteristics above together.

Companies can copy that model and try to innovate like the best companies in the world. However, I have noticed this top-down strategy is not enough.

If you are into business, you must have heard this quote, often attributed to Peter Drucker: "Culture eats strategy for breakfast" (Engel, 2018). This means you can set whatever course you want for your business, but it will be your culture—what your people believe and how they behave—that determines what will live out in work. In his book, *Thirteeners: Why Only 13 Percent of Companies Successfully Execute Their Strategy—and How Yours Can Be One of Them*, Daniel F. Prosser highlights that strategy is not the issue. It's about the execution made by the people working at the firm.

The most important thing is that employees should act with a perfect alignment of its strategy so their ideas can be implemented. After that, if we want to create an innovation DNA, we need more people to think as they do in startups. Those are the individuals with the entrepreneurial mindset who are capable of tapping into their network to solve problems. They do things cheaper, fail faster, and often work with agile methodologies.

Companies believe they have to put new rules to force employees to behave in a certain way, but change happens when it is both ways: top-down and bottom-up, coming from the employees themselves. Most efforts from the leadership are to tell employees what to do instead of creating an environment where people are fearless, hopeful, collaborative, engaged in their day everyday work activities, and take the initiative.

Companies will interact with external partners more and more in the coming years. Working in ecosystems and networks can overcome obstacles such as slow execution, lack of IP, or experts to build new technology. Amid the uncertainty, employees can tap into their internal or external networks to make better decisions, improve their ideas, and access data and information. Today, the people who do not learn to collaborate and do not have the right mindset will rapidly become frustrated, unhappy, disappointed, and unsuccessful. The new workforce must learn how to collaborate smarter and more efficiently.

Those who do will have an unfair advantage and have a much more significant positive impact on the world. This book will teach the mindset shift to use today's fast-changing world superpower: building networks.

Some of the following terms will be explained more deeply in the next chapter. In brief, the difference between how corporations operated in the old economy compared to the how they will operate in the future economy is set out as follows:

Old Economy:

- Highly structured days and projects with timelines and processes
- Replicability is the main goal for large-scale manufacturing
- Short-term driven, focused on quarterly reporting.
- Vertical structure of business units
- Very rigid hierarchies,
- Disciplined workforce following rules and not welcome to challenge them.
- R&D department working in silos.
- Almost no startups

Future Economy:

- Agile, fast-moving, and adaptable
- Purpose-driven, solving a more significant problem as the primary goal
- Ecosystem driven, multistakeholder with a focus on collaboration
- Focused on long term, through partnerships
- Flat hierarchies
- Employees are welcome to challenge the status quo
- Less R&D, more collaboration with startups
- High receptivity to startups and entrepreneurs

The next chapter will discuss how some innovators made discoveries by reaching out to their networks, how companies can be more agile, how networks work, and why they are so effective.

<u>*TAKE ACTION:*</u>

Be part of the change and decide to lead it. This starts by defining the problem you are trying to solve and why you are doing it.

Understand the different stakeholders of your ecosystem, and start building relationships with them.

If you're part of an organization working with startups, push your company to apply key mindset principles presented in this book to make the ecosystem more collaborative and effective.

If you part of a company, do not hesitate to challenge the management. Today's change is not only top down, but also bottom up. More in the upcoming chapters.

CHAPTER 2

Networks Work; Here Is Why

"Your network is your net worth."

—*TIM SANDERS*

In 2015, I visited the Dead Vlei (or "dead marsh" in English) in Namibia, where you can observe the dead trees in the middle of the desert. Some 900 years ago the climate dried up, and dunes moved from their original positions, which cut off Dead Vlei from the river. They died because they were disconnected from the ecosystems and lost access to water. A tree can grow on its own. It can even survive alone in a desert. It's possible. But nothing can *thrive* if isolated. Even alone, the tree has a network, if only a very small one with limited resources. If the tree is in a forest, it would have much more resources at its disposal.

The same happens in life and business. Growth cannot be sustained over time. Connection with others is a necessity and has never been so powerful and effective in today's fast-moving and interdisciplinary world. A single person can start a company, but that company won't be able to sustain the change and crisis over time if it doesn't collaborate and form networks.

My mentor Rama would tell me, "The more sparks you create, the more likely you are to catch a fire." If we equate the spark to a person, it is straightforward. One person can start a metaphorical fire—a revolution, for example. But there are two problems. Firstly, on one's own, it can take forever to start the fire, and secondly, the fire may not last long. However, with more sparks (i.e., more people), the fire can be made instantly, and it will last longer.

Like me, many others would like to wake up in the morning and feel we're part of a positive change.

In the past, companies focused on their profits and value chains. This way of doing things was an old inside-out thinking, which didn't start from actual customer pains. This model cannot solve our world's vast problems.

What we need is to see the big picture and tackle systemic issues together. Companies that embrace the collaborative model have shown the world it works. If you talk about this with people, you'll quickly get into a debate about how to innovate, how to have ideas, how to implement ideas, and so forth. In my opinion, there is one solution to all these points: networks. On both an individual and a societal level, the solution to overcome obstacles, solve problems, and create wealth for those driving meaningful change lies in networks.

We do not have any choice; we now live in a multistakeholder economy, and it is here to stay.

By networks, I mean more than just the "networking" concept we may refer to in the business world, like going to a networking event and having drinks with people. Networks involve connecting previously unrelated dots (knowledge areas) to solve a problem that cannot be solved in isolation. When I use the word *network* in this book, I mean:

1. Network of knowledge and ideas: to be inspired, test hypotheses, and improve your project, product, goal.
2. Network of resources such as capital (as revenue, debt, equity, grant financing), infrastructure for your dream company or project, legal support, marketing opportunities, administrative, databases with critical information, etc.
3. Network of people to join you full time, work with you, and help you accomplish your goals, vision, and mission.

This chapter highlights the fact that in the past, with hierarchies and decisions power coming from the top, we did not use them effectively. However, data and research point out we need them. Let us start with the network of knowledge.

NETWORK OF KNOWLEDGE: HOW TO BECOME A BETTER INNOVATOR AND INVENTOR

Kevin Dunbard, a psychologist at McGill University, studied scientists to understand how they made their discoveries. In the early 1990s, he decided to take a new approach to scientific discovery. Instead of reading biographies and asking scientists how they made their discoveries, he decided to simply watch them as they worked. He set up cameras in their labs and recorded as much as possible. In addition to that, he also interviewed them about the advancement of their research. Dunbard found scientists changed their strategy and tried a new experience based on their discussion with other scientists. More importantly, Dunbard discovered the best ideas emerged during regular lab meetings. Dozens of researchers would gather and informally present and discuss their latest work. The "distributed reasoning," where several scientists come together to understand and solve a problem, distinguished the successful scientists from the others. Innovation did not come from the microscope but rather from the conference table (Weiss, 1998)!

Receiving feedback from others was what made these scientists successful. When colleagues asked new questions, with different reasoning, etc., it often recontextualized a problem. The larger your network—with various ideas coming from other places—the more well-rounded your argument will be. The lab meetings created a place for ideas to collide, where new combinations could be formed, and where information flowed from one project to the next. Working alone can trap your thoughts in your initial bias and make you "blind" about essential things to consider. The social flow of a group turns good ideas into transformative ideas. So, reach out to your colleagues and ask for input!

As Steven Johnson mentions it in his book, *Where Good Ideas Come From,* "Many of history's great innovators managed to build a cross-disciplinary coffeehouse environment within their private work routines."

In the book, *The Sociology of Philosophies: A Global Theory of Intellectual Change*, Randall Collins analyzed the network of philosophers and mathematicians over two thousand years in both Asian and Western societies. He concluded the individual's network and the ability of a person to tap into their social capital to gather ideas were the secret behind their exceptional creativity.

However, most employees in today's corporate world try to solve problems on their own and only ask questions of their direct manager. Even after decades of "corporate innovation renaissance" it is still very difficult, if not impossible, for many organizations to open up their innovation process between the silos of the organization.

THE PROBLEM: THE TRADITIONAL TOP-DOWN AP-PROACH GETS IN THE WAY OF NETWORKS

All design thinking classes will teach us about the power of asking questions of your customer. For a real-life example of this, I turned to LinkedIn and posted the question, "Who would like to be interviewed and discuss networks for my book?" Stuart Gregg reached out. The topic of changing the way we do things appealed to him, so we had a chat.

Stuart is an operation and innovation professional with over twenty years of specialist experience in the energy sector working with operators, service providers, and startups. Stuart has been through everything where change was needed, from the oil industry to sustainability (hydrogen, carbon capture, etc.) and digital products. He comes in to change technology, redesign processes, and provide robust solutions for poor-performing businesses process utilization. During our interview, this change-maker told me about some of the innovation projects he had been involved with.

In 2006, Stuart was working on a project on an offshore installation to exploit petroleum and natural gas. On the platform, the operators had to do daily checks on machinery and equipment, and they used pen and paper to note down the machines' functioning or signal a defect. Stuart and his team wanted to remove manual and non-digital ways of doing things because it was open to human error, and there was no data collection. They imagined an operator entering all the information on an industrial tablet to measure or control the pressure, temperature, etc. The operator could use an RFID card to log in with a simple tap and enter the data into the system. Once back into the office, the operator would log on to the computer and visualize the data, capture trends, analytics, and so forth.

What Stuart and his team envisioned failed miserably.

The first reason it failed was it didn't involve enough end-users to use the system. They didn't have the end-users' buy-in to use this system; the operators felt they were forced to use it. Secondly, the new process contained too many steps. Before, it was a two-step process: writing the status of the equipment down while checking, then typing the results into a spreadsheet back in the office. The new approach was five steps. "Straight away, we lost the workforce," Stuart said. "They couldn't see how this was more efficient; they didn't see it improving what they had always done. And to be fair to them, they were correct." Importantly, Stuart admitted their novel innovation didn't improve the accuracy because there's no fundamental difference between them jotting the information down with pen and paper and looking at a screen and then typing it in.

This is an example of traditional innovation, a top-down approach, and processes. Top management thinks of something then tells the guys what they should or should not do. Today, the companies that do this, in the management space or even product innovation, fail.

When a person comes up with a good idea, it comes from having had many different experiences, and the magic lies in combining these experiences. Ask your customers the right questions, so you truly understand the underlying pain or question instead of getting improved versions of the current solution they know. And ask many of them! Customers who use the products have many experiences and can share the best insights. Bouncing ideas back and forth between you and your customers and clients or your friends, family, and colleagues is the best way to get the *best* idea. So why do companies try to establish processes and isolate people on projects and tell them what to do in a structured way when we know it doesn't work in the world of rapid and intense change?

When I entered the corporate world as a young professional, I always questioned the rationale behind having hierarchies. Why do people at the top make decisions about the things they sometimes have no clue about? Why would project leaders not be project based, depending on their experience and expertise on a given topic? I have also witnessed the information doesn't flow appropriately across teams because of the necessity to go through the top of the pyramid. Furthermore, when someone needs help, they don't go through their network to ask for information and support; they just ask their boss, who often can't help anyway. This kills innovation, and I am not a fan of it. The place for exchange as described in Kevin Dunbard's experiment above can't work in such an environment.

Too much control and too many restrictions can potentially sap a brilliant mind's best ideas. However, hierarchies are here for a reason and will probably stay for a while. Consider this:

- In his book, *Thinking, Fast and Slow*, Daniel Kahneman—psychologist, behavioral economist, and Nobel laureate—says the human mind rejects complexity in the world in favor of simplicity.
- Our world is full of unpredictable events. According to research published in *The Journal of Neuroscience,* "unpredictability is sufficient to induce sustained neural activity in the amygdala and to elicit anxiety-like behavior" (Herry et al., 2007). We humans will unconsciously try to make things "predictable" to avoid a sense of fear.
- As Nir Eyal, author of the book, *Hooked: How to Build Habit-forming Products*, writes in his article on motivation, all behavior is prompted by a desire to escape discomfort. Everything we do is about the need for homeostasis to restore psychological balance (Nir and Far, 2022).
- According to Brad Feld and Ian Hathaway in their book, *The Startup Community Way: Evolving an Entrepreneurial*

Ecosystem, companies used to work in hierarchies, which was suitable for tight control of production, information, and resources.

- People looking for processes and structures are linear system thinkers; they avoid diversity, making predictive models more challenging and harder to calibrate and maintain. Networks are complex systems, but there, variety is of central importance. It builds resilience and produces different outputs and results (Page, 2017).

The points above demonstrate people and companies avoid the power of networks due to their complexity and the need to feel "in control." Humans always try to simplify complex systems, so we love our traditional hierarchical model, even in innovation teams.

I insist we should reduce hierarchies. Working in networks will encourage bold thinking and maximize interaction with the external world. Networks promote the possibility of working with the most talented individuals, who are not afraid of failure but accept it as part of the learning process and tackle big problems. These people are interdisciplinarians and visionaries (Ishak, 2017). This is why we should consider inviting everyone we work with to consider a "top-down-bottom-up" approach.

THE SOLUTION: TODAY'S CHANGE COMES FROM A "TOP-DOWN-BOTTOM-UP" APPROACH ENABLED BY FEWER HIERARCHIES AND AGILE, MULTIDISCIPLINARY TEAMS

Having fewer hierarchies can work by introducing more agile teams. As described in the 2018 *Harvard Business Review* article, "Agile at Scale," "agile teams are usually small and multidisciplinary. Once confronted with large and complex problems, the teams break into modules" (Rigby, Sutherland, and Noble, 2018). The agile teams develop solutions to each problem through rapid prototyping and tight feedback loops. As a core principle, the team prioritizes adapting to change over sticking to an established plan. Those teams are the ones best suited for innovation.

I love this approach. In today's fast-evolving world, the probability we land on a project away from our core expertise is high. Why should some people always be the leader of the projects? It simply doesn't make sense. Let's say you want to launch a new marketing initiative to promote your team. Young people may be a better fit to lead a social media project than someone with twenty-plus years of experience who doesn't understand the world of social media. If I am a scientist and the project is about building a back- and front-end software for traffic control, maybe I should pass the lead on to someone else. However, if the project is about controlling water quality in Africa, I'm your man because I have studied the minerals present in water. I have traveled to eight countries in Africa that suffer from lack of proper infrastructure. As I have some experience in it, I may be the right fit to lead the team.

An article on the blog, *Agile Radicals,* explains how Spotify introduced the terms "tribes," "chapters," and "guilds" to replace heads and teams with temporary staff based on the project size and skills needed. This is the way to go, and it works.

Darrell Rigby and his colleagues have studied the scaling up of agile teams at hundreds of companies. They found companies like Spotify and Netflix run their entire organization with agile, networked, matrixed teams. Other very innovative companies, such as Amazon, Google, Bosch, and SAP, use a mix of hierarchies and agile teams (Rigby, 2018).

In this new model, as leadership can lie not only at the top but also at the bottom, the exchange of fruitful ideas and the flow of information occurs faster between stakeholders. However, many cultures are still against that new way of working because it entails questioning everything, challenging the status quo (including your boss), and being transparent with other teams inside and outside your organization. However, this new approach helps the information flow horizontally and brings more people into the project's mission. Therefore, change is more likely to occur. To understanding why it is so effective and necessary, let's look at some real-life examples.

NETWORK OF RESOURCES: LEARNING FROM-REAL LIFE EXAMPLES

I have often walked through a forest and looked at the birds, insects, and trees. What we see in nature is more dependent on each other than we may at first realize. For instance, the mycelium network of mushrooms is a great way to understand the power of networks. We have all seen mush-rooms on the ground, but have you seen the other part of the mushroom, the part living underground? That part goes very deep underground. The mushroom's "roots" interact and connect with tree roots as a vast network. This network transfers water, nitrogen, carbon, and other minerals to indi-vidual plants. The more extensive and denser those networks are, the healthier the forest is. Those networks are called the mycelium networks (Fricker et al., 2017). A similar astonish-ing network can be found in sequoia forests in California. Its biggest tree, the "General Sherman," stands eighty-three feet (275 meters) tall and is over thirty-six feet (eleven meters) in diameter at the base. This tree is estimated to be between 2,000 and 2,700 years old. The root of the sequoia trees typically grows around eleven to fourteen feet (two to five meters) deep (Monumental Trees, 2022). The roots of these trees spread 150 to 200 feet (over fifty meters) and intertwine with others to create a mesh that literally stands the test of time. The mushrooms or sequoia tree build is what makes forests withstand powerful winds and droughts.

Similarly, humans depend on each other to thrive and grow, and when we are with others, we can exchange valuable resources. Humans have been detaching and separating into smaller groups for thousands of years. In ancient times, on a societal level, looking for a community (networking-wise) was a matter of life or death, and that need to belong is still deeply rooted in our brain.

With the rise of the industrial revolution, corporations enabled humans to collaborate in groups larger than one hundred members. Also, more people started moving to cities, which became bigger and bigger, year after year. I experienced the power of cities firsthand. I grew up in a small village in France with a thousand inhabitants, and later, I went to study and work in major cities such as Zurich in Switzerland, San Francisco in the United States, and now Berlin, Germany. In those cities, I met people who inspired me to do new projects and improve my career outlook.

I was curious about whether being in a city helps one to be more creative? In my research I found several studies and books that talk about this. Like the mycelium network of mushrooms that transfer vital resources to trees and plants, cities accelerate innovation by enabling the exchange of resources among its population. Cities make people interact, which helps them learn, build on each other, and grow. Cities are considered key environments for the emergence of innovative interactions and relationships. This is why creative and innovative industries tend to localize in vibrant urban environments; so, people can exchange knowledge and connect with experts, specialized suppliers, designers, customers, and workers to create new products and services (Concilio et al., 2018).

It is no surprise that innovation and startups were built in significant hubs where not only the creative individuals but also all necessary stakeholders to build businesses could be found. Such well-known seats are San Francisco, New York, and Boston in the US. In Europe, most startups also come from significant hubs such as London, Paris, and Berlin.

In the end, innovation and change will happen when there is a culture and a way of thinking that promotes it. Let's continue with my conversation with Stuart from the beginning of this chapter. He and his team had the best intentions to create change on the offshore installation in 2006 but failed due to the wrong process. A few years later, they worked differently.

NETWORK OF PEOPLE AND THE SUCCESS OF A MULTISTAKEHOLDER, TRANSPARENT, BOTTOM-UP APPROACH

In 2013, Stuart's team managed a messy warehousing and distribution system. This time, they used a different approach on a new project. They wanted to streamline the process and make it more digital, so here's what they did.

They brought the different teams together in a room: the guys who bought the equipment, the guys who stored the equipment, and the guys who distributed it. Stuart's team told them to draw the current process on a whiteboard. Interestingly, they drew with different processes despite the fact it should be one and the same one. The project team asked the participants, "If we could make this completely digital, with your wildest ideas, what would it look like?"

Over the next two days, the participants drew a new process inspired by the massive German supermarket chain, Aldi. They asked themselves, "How does Aldi manage their materials? How do they ensure that the shelf is always full of soup?"

After the workshop, Stuart's team engaged with several specialists in that field, people who had been involved with supermarkets in the past. They got the right technology, and they ran a pilot at one installation with the team that designed the process. After going through the alpha and beta stages to iron out the issues, the group launched a three-month pilot at three different sites. They took the data about what worked and what didn't work, and, as a next step, they came up with an action plan to remove what didn't work. They highlighted this information and communicated it further within the business.

Before they did the full rollout, they asked the original team who designed the system to run workshops with the operational on-site teams to deploy it at the new installations. By showing the people who had experience in that area had designed and tested the process and were also involved with rolling it out, they got buy-in from the local operations teams. This whole project took about twelve months, and at its conclusion, the procedure was automated end-to-end at twenty-five installations.

Stuart's team had achieved excellent results over three years through the successful implementation of this project. They reduced the loss of material by 60 percent, and the amount they spent on their materials dropped by 30 percent. Finally, the number of breakdowns of equipment that could be fixed within one day increased by 60 percent. This was because they had the right spares in the right place at the right time. The system learned as it was going—what was needed and where it was needed—and would advise you accordingly.

We learned from Stuart that if you want to create a change in your team or organization, you cannot apply the past model of innovation—acting on the instructions and requests of leadership without question. Stuart's innovation project failed in 2006 due to the top-down approach. In 2013, they put all the *right* people, a multidisciplinary team selected based on the necessary background and experience, not title, in the room and brainstormed ideas. The magic was in the feedback loop. It connected previous unrelated dots (the storage system of the offshore installation and the German grocery stores storage system) and used the bottom-up approach. In the end, we can call it a "top-down-bottom-up" approach, which means everybody has to be involved. It's about the network of insights collected from the different stakeholders. There, the information traveled freely across the stakeholders, and they worked with the "right" third-party technology provider, who had dealt with this problem in the past. It is also important to mention we need the right project managers, the ones capable of dealing with this new approach. The ones who can put their ego to the side to help everyone exchange ideas and to welcome feedback.

CONCLUSION

The network approach works to get new ideas, access resources, or attract people to join the project. Furthermore, networks provide support and, to a degree, encourage risk, with different viewpoints adding to knowledge levels, thereby mitigating risk as a group (more about resilience in Chapter 8). Granted, the reality of this network model is messier and often comes with unpredictable outcomes. This way of working and living is not easy to digest, and that's why most organizations perceive this as a risk. Still, future-ready organizations should be committed to creative disruption, embrace technological collision, and use unpredictability to drive innovation and change.

However, the power of networks is not equal everywhere, and its efficiency depends on the behavior of people participating in the network. One of the ways to make those networks even more effective is to have diverse teams (more about this in Chapters 5 and 6), and having people embrace a collaborative mindset. Places like Boston, Silicon Valley, and even Israel is well known for their economic output, innovation capacity, and ability to not sink in a crisis or extreme change. They simply adapt, embrace the difference, and become even more successful. I was fortunate to work and live for in San Francisco for a year. I witnessed six things they are doing differently. Let's explore this in Chapter 3.

TAKE ACTION:

Create an environment to maximize serendipity and opportunities. Make people come together to exchange ideas. If you can, build a live or virtual cross-disciplinary coffeehouse. Do this through formal ways, but also make sure informal gatherings and idea/experience exchange is facilitated and encouraged.

Anytime you need help dealing with obstacles, reach out to your network. Remember, the more extensive your network, the greater your superpower. Don't always reach out to the same people; that can be annoying.

If you're not familiar with agile methodologies and agile teams, ask your network to understand it better, as it will be implemented widely across organizations.

Make the shift from hierarchies to agile teams to make more people take initiative (bottom-up). If you are a junior in the organization, propose this new model to your boss.

Maximize the flow of information with the right stakeholders and establish a feedback loop with a network that should be as diverse as possible. Test your ideas, experiment, and make more people active and engaged in the projects.

CHAPTER 3

Six Things Silicon Valley Is Doing Right

———

"Silicon Valley is a mindset, not a location."

—REID HOFFMAN, FOUNDER OF LINKEDIN

I've often asked this question, either in online polls or directly to entrepreneurs: "What are the most important things to make any business a success?" The answers were invariably the same: firstly, people, and secondly, mindset.

Silicon Valley is famous for its vast economic successes. As an article in *The Guardian* puts it, "If Silicon Valley were a country, it would be among the richest on earth." Silicon Valley earns $128,308 per capita annually in gross domestic product; its residents outproduce almost every nation on the planet (Pulkkinen, 2019). The StartupBlink report, "Global Startup Ecosystem Rankings 2021," ranked ecosystems of 1,000 cities and one hundred countries. They refrained from using subjective tools such as surveys and interviews, and instead utilized data either accumulated directly from the StartupBlink map or arrived from their data partners such as CB Insights, TechCrunch, etc. Using artificial intelligence and algorithms, a final total score was generated to represent the innovation output and the startups they generate, in terms of quantity and quality. It found San Francisco and Silicon Valley outperforms the rest of the world in terms of both the number of startups and innovations. San Francisco Bay (Silicon Valley) was ranked first with a total score of 328,966. New York was second (110,777), followed by Beijing (66,749), Los Angeles (58,441), London (56,913), and Boston (49.835). Tel Aviv ranked eighth, Paris eleventh, and Berlin thirteenth, out of thousands of cities. While this is just one study with a specific algorithm, it nevertheless shows how advanced the region is.

So, why is Silicon Valley so successful? Why does it continue to innovate so much more than the rest of the world, year after year? Many cities or regions worldwide are trying, unsuccessfully, to replicate this success. What is the secret? In this chapter, I will endeavor to explain, based on my experience living and working in Silicon Valley for a year. (Note that I lived there pre-COVID, and things may have changed a bit.)

So, how did I get an internship in Silicon Valley with absolutely no business skills? I tried to apply for online jobs, but nobody answered. I knew I had to find another way, so I started reaching out directly to people I found in journal papers and news articles, and I asked people I knew to make an introduction. After a top executive of a French company made an intro for me, I finally got an interview with Rama

Penta (at that time, director) and Dirk Schapeler (at that time vice president of digital transformation, leading the Silicon Valley Office).

In the interview, Dirk asked me, "Why should we hire you when we can hire people from the University of Berkeley or Stanford more easily?" (As a European, getting a visa to work in the United States is quite complicated and challenging.) Not an easy question to answer. I certainly wasn't going to reply, "Because I'm better than them." Instead, I said I wanted to go there to learn entrepreneurship and be involved with the latest technologies and trends.

A few years later I asked Rama why they decided to hire me. He said it was because I networked without any fear; I reached out to Dirk in person. They loved the approach. "We were looking for someone in life science and IT background. Based on your energy, open-mindedness, and flexible thinking, we figured you weren't molded into a specific way of thinking but rather could be entrepreneurial. We know this area can be ambiguous and felt you could do well with our direction. We felt Bay Area would help your career more than others."

I finally joined the digital health accelerator of Bayer, the German multinational pharmaceutical and life sciences company, without having any hard skills needed for the job. Their hiring decision already shows how they think. They hired based on attitude, mindset and not skills. Let's now explore six major things they are doing right.

THE 6 CHARACTERISTICS OF SILICON VALLEY

To help me make sense of my experience in Silicon Valley, I turned to Deepti Pahwa. A Stanford Graduate School of Business alumni, Deepti is a founding partner of LISA (Lead Incubator and Startup Accelerator). She has worked at the intersection of innovation, brand strategy, and human-centered design for nearly twenty years. Her experience spans multiple industries, from chief innovation officer of Contakt World (a health tech startup in Silicon Valley) and working on pandemic technologies with MIT Media Labs, to leading Product Design and Brand Strategy for Global Lifestyle Brands (which includes the likes of Calvin Klein, Swatch Group, Zalando, and Swarovski).

Deepti was born in India and lived in Germany and Switzerland for more than sixteen years. Like me, she noticed how the approach to innovation and entrepreneurship in Europe is wildly different from Silicon Valley. Together we brainstormed six characteristics of Silicon Valley that makes it so successful:

1. They have a moonshot mindset
2. They fail fast, often, and forward
3. They have a culture of mentorship
4. They have an event culture
5. They grow as communities and networks by sharing
6. They have a well-coalesced ecosystem

Let's look at each in detail.

1. THE MOONSHOT MINDSET: THEY THINK BIG

As mentioned at the beginning of the chapter, people and mindset are essential for business success. In Europe and most of the world, people are afraid to take significant risks. However, not in Silicon Valley. Silicon Valley's culture can be described as the moonshot mindset. "Moonshot" is a term used to describe a lofty goal requiring monumental effort—in other words, a giant leap (Merriam-Webster, 2022). An example of this is the Human Genome Project, a three-billion-dollar, fifteen-year effort to map the approximately 100,000 human genes. As we can only scratch the surface of this topic here, I'm going to focus on the mindsets of Silicon Valley's investors and entrepreneurs.

INVESTORS

In the Mindvalley online course, "The Power of Boldness," well-known entrepreneur Naveen Jain talks about the importance of mindset when building a business. He specifically refers to the investor mindset of Silicon Valley, as opposed to the rest of the world. If he pitched the idea of launching a rocket to the moon, Silicon Valley investors would reply, "Tell me more; how would you do this?" However, most investors from elsewhere would say, "Please don't waste my time; get out." If your idea is too big or bold, they won't hear you out.

A biotech startup founder I worked with during my time in Silicon Valley confirmed this. When he pitched an idea to a Silicon Valley venture capital (VC) firm in a fundraising meeting, they asked, "If we give you one billion dollars, what will you do with it?" He was shocked and realized he wasn't sufficiently prepared to answer that question.

Investors in Silicon Valley don't want to just give you money. They want you to transform society. This is also why entrepreneurs think differently. The money is widely available in the region, but not only that. The risk capital is probably the most important driver of an ecosystem—and this availability of money is tied to the investment and portfolio mindset of VC-backed innovation. Silicon Valley's VCs have the mindset for productive failure, and this builds robust portfolios (if one in ten investments works, it is still a profitable business).

ENTREPRENEURS

Entrepreneurs think in terms of transformative ideas that most people deem impossible. As Peter Diamandis, an entrepreneur best known as the founder and chairman of the XPRIZE Foundation and co-founder and executive chairman of Singularity University, puts it, "The day before something is a breakthrough, it's a crazy idea." (Diamandis, 2012).

By definition, entrepreneurs *need* to think beyond today, and they also behave differently. It's okay if most people don't understand your idea right away. Entrepreneurs have a big vision about what the world looks like in five or even ten years. Having a big vision comes with a growth mindset and willingness to fall and learn from failures.

2. FAIL FAST, FAIL OFTEN, FAIL FORWARD

It's no secret that one of the defining characteristics of Silicon Valley is its high failure rate. And that's exactly where growth is found—on the other end of the failure. And that leads to vitality and the generation of new wealth. Failure unleashes future growth and success. Knowing we are allowed to fail gives us the freedom to experiment without being constrained by the fear of failure.

The most significant difference between Europe and Silicon Valley is the mindset that allows for failure without judgment. In Europe, there is an atmosphere of fear of failure. It's common to see pockets of innovation that do not share the Silicon Valley mindset toward failure also do not place a high social value on entrepreneurship. The society is more conservative, which results in less innovation. The result of this culture is that there is less investment in transformational companies.

Revenue first, or growth first? Startup companies in the US compete in a big market and need a high degree of market penetration to gain a competitive advantage. Hence, investors and startup founders alike see growth and traction as the main success factors. In comparison, with less later-stage funding available, European startups cannot afford to spend as much on growth, instead needing to generate revenue earlier to stay alive. And this hinders the culture of failure; the decision for a startup is often between continuing to keep active or embracing loss (with the exception of biotech and pharma startups, where the funding process is different and more complex).

One of the things I realized during my time in Silicon Valley is that people are more okay with failing because they are supported by their network—including their mentors.

3. THE MENTORSHIP CULTURE: THE MINDSET OF GIVING BACK

When I arrived in San Francisco, I received an excellent onboarding. On my first day, my manager, Rama Penta, whom I mentioned earlier, took me for lunch to a wonderful Ethiopian restaurant (we both remember it so well). He asked, "What do you want to learn here? What are your expectations? How can we make your time here the most incredible time ever?"

For the first three weeks, Rama took an hour every day to explain to me—in a one-to-one setting—something about the pharmaceutical industry; how it works, entrepreneurship, business, the market, and more. That onboarding enabled me to get up to speed in record time. He also urged me to accept two fundamental principles: "Mikel, you need to be comfortable with what is uncomfortable. And you have to be able to handle ambiguity."

Because he helped me so much, he became much more than a boss; he became my mentor, friend, and someone I can count on when I have issues. To this day we still talk and message each other. For instance, I recently had a challenging experience at work and complained about it. He said to me, "The day you don't learn, or you're not stretched, is the day you have to change your job." This helped me reframe my problems.

This mentality of giving back—where senior executives help and guide young people—is what successful people do in Silicon Valley. Why? Because they experienced it themselves when they were young, and now they want to do the same. They give it back to the community.

How do you get a mentor? It starts by asking questions. We—young people—are afraid to ask questions because we tend to think these experienced and senior individuals are so busy. I have realized the more we ask meaningful questions and repeatedly ask until they reply, the more likely it is they will take the time to mentor us. They don't help if we don't ask anything. Once we show we're ambitious and looking forward to achieving something big, they will take the time to help us.

We've all had a situation in our life where we met a person who radically changed the trajectory of our life. Maybe we met that person once or many times over a period of time. This happens in Silicon Valley all the time. Serendipity.

4. THE EVENT CULTURE: MAXIMIZING SERENDIPITY

When building a business, we deal with a million things we don't know. That's one of the things that make entrepreneurship so hard. One of the best ways to overcome the obstacles in your way is to know the people who deal with the same problems as you and those who are good at different areas of interest than you are.

During my twelve months in Silicon Valley, I went to over 120 events—sometimes after work, sometimes during my working hours if it was related to my job. The people I met there were fun, open, and ready to help. You connect with high energy, talented, individuals by going *and* participating.

People share and give their feedback on, ideas, pitches, or whatever they are working on.

Some of the events I attended include:

- Product launch seminars with the likes of Adobe's product manager and Microsoft's experienced professionals
- Entrepreneurship stories and round table discussions related to failure, fundraising, or working with corporates
- A pitch practice event and actual pitches in front of investors
- Industry-specific meetups—for example, 3D printing, stem cells, etc.
- A "meet our startups" event at an accelerator/incubator
- Networking events, getting to know the people in my industry

One of the reasons people move to San Francisco is to network and build relationships. I experienced that after going to a few events and seeing the same people. If they like you, these people start inviting you to their private parties. This happened to me; I was invited to "invitation only" parties. At these parties you get to meet the actual drivers and business influencers of Silicon Valley: millionaires and billionaires, serial entrepreneurs, and people highly ranked in society.

At one particular private event, I sat among *New York Times* best-selling authors, people working with Michelle Obama, and even a member of the royal family of Luxembourg. After dinner, we went to a private club you could only enter if someone in the club knew you. You not only have great conversations at these events, it's also where real business happens. Genuine partnerships are made right in the club around music and drinks.

I have seen startups succeed because the CEO could make great connections. VCs invest in the team, not the idea or the technology. Everyone knows that a company can only be successful if great people are running it. Even if this is not specific to Silicon Valley anymore, they initiated this way of doing business.

But networks are not built on day one. Everyone should start very early, before you lead a major initiative. It's too late to start making important connections when you need it. You can get started by reaching out for a coffee chat (virtual or live) and simply getting to know each other. Or going to a conference and asking questions to the speaker afterward.

It is all about people.

5. COMMUNITIES AND NETWORKS: TO CONNECT WITH SHARED VALUE AND PURPOSE

People in Silicon Valley come across new faces daily. They work in the same industry, and they will help others who have the same problems. Most people enjoy sharing what they have learned and giving advice to other entrepreneurs. Nobody is hiding; everybody is sharing. This increases their chance of meeting the person who will transform and impact their lives. Serendipity is at its maximum. Thanks to their extensive network, most of the time you could get an introduction to someone that may be able to help you. It is also good to know there is a high chance you'll sit next to your next Angel investor who will fund your next big idea.

Networks don't form by themselves. What makes this region different from other places is its ability to be proactive and make those connections (more about this in Chapter 4). CEOs usually join communities like 3DHeals, StartupHealth, InnovatorMD, and the German American Business Association (GABA), to name a few. Often, they enter the community because they resonate with the purpose and mission, which makes it easier to bond with people. They feel part of something bigger.

6. A WELL-COALESCED ECOSYSTEM: CONNECTING ALL PLAYERS

Silicon Valley has two major components that makes it connected and robust:

1. They have the talent and infrastructure (startups, investors, venture capital funds, top-ranked universities, and medical centers, providers of support services (e.g., legal, accounting, etc.), mature companies to scale technologies, or regional and state organizations).
2. They have a willingness to interact, collaborate, and thrive together.

In January 2021, I interviewed Gregory Theyel, the founder of the Biomedical Manufacturing Network (Mikel Mangold, 2021). His organization is on a mission to understand the need of a company, detect how they fit in the network, and how they can benefit from it.

Greg works with different companies but mostly tries to help small ones with five to fifty employees. These small companies usually identify a problem or develop a particular piece of technology. Still, they are not aware of many things. For example:

- How to connect with a contract manufacturer
- Where to find a specific type of adhesive
- Which sensor to choose

"I feel there is a perception that people can just google something and find the answer, but it's not quite true. In most cases, it's the specialty insight that a network can provide. Without it, it becomes an important missing piece of the puzzle," shared Greg.

His organization is funded by the government, with the purpose of connecting people, connecting a big company with a startup or a university with mature companies. They make those essential connections to these larger systems.

As a reminder, anyone and every company on this planet today needs to work with multiple stakeholders. We're in the era of the "multistakeholder economy." If you want to implement a new product or idea on the market, or even if you want to create a non-profit that can change the world, the network is a critical success factor. The more you're connected, or in a position to ask for an introduction, the greater the chance you will be able to implement your idea.

CONCLUSION

The six characteristics described above may feel simplistic to describe what the Bay Area is all about. Indeed, many have written entire books about it and gone deeper into details and analysis. However, this chapter illustrates what I and many others have experienced by living and working there. The goal of this chapter was to set the foundation of the message of this book: It's about people, networks, and mindset.

Silicon Valley succeeds as a network. It brings everyone together in a melting pot. What really differentiates Silicon Valley from other places of innovation is the density per square meter of people trying to change the world and their willingness to make introductions. It's their mindset. This curiosity, the bold thinking, their risk capital, the network of people, the variety of stakeholders, and their ambition to use ideas to transform society; these are the things that make Silicon Valley the father of entrepreneurship and the best entrepreneurial city in the world.

By reading this, I hope you will feel inspired to implement some of these points above in your city, anywhere in the world, to build an entrepreneurial ecosystem.

In the next part of this book, we will dig deeper into the Seven Mindset Principles required to build, participate and benefit from networks.

TAKE ACTION:

Mindset: The best way to change your mindset is to work with people who have that moonshot mindset. (A great way to start this mindset shift would be to read Peter Diamandis' and Steve Kotler's books, BOLD and The Future Is Faster Than You Think.) If you hire people, just observe how they asked questions to tell how flexible their thinking is.

Failure: Find a way to work with people who promote it, embrace it, and make everyone in the team feel that failure is normal.

Mentorship: If you are a senior executive reading this, please consider reserving time in your schedule to help motivate young people. It will have a huge impact on their careers. If you are a young professional, be fearless, reach out to top executives, and ask your questions.

Event and communities: Depending on where you are in the world, find your groups and communities using platforms like Meetup, Eventbrite, Slack, and Facebook. If you go, make a good impression. It is all about the law of resonance. You attract the energy you generate. Make sure to smile, ask interesting questions, and find ways to help them, and they will want to invite you and collaborate with you

Ecosystem: In major innovation ecosystems, you will often find what is called a "backbone organization." In Boston, it is the Massachusetts Life Sciences Center. In Basel, Switzerland, it is the Basel Area Business and Innovation. Find out what networking infrastructure your city has to connect you to the right people.

PART 2

SEVEN MINDSET PRINCIPLES TO BUILD, JOIN, OR LEVERAGE THE POWER OF NETWORKS

CHAPTER 4

Principle 1: DO-IT-YOURSELF, Take Ownership

—

"Build a network to magnify your company."

Let's be honest; unless you're Elon Musk, Bill Gates, Ariana Huffington, or Michelle Obama, your network won't build itself. Nobody will do it for you when you start your career. This chapter is about how you can be proactive in building it. I have always been curious why some people can create multiple successful companies and keep doing it, and others fail repeatedly. After doing some research, I have concluded the most valuable skill in business is not how good you are at doing research at your desk but rather your ability to gather people around a shared intention. The world's most prominent change-makers are superheroes at building networks.

In his book, Brad Feld, the co-founder of Techstars, mentioned an estimated half of the new ventures are started by teams, with founders recruited from their networks. "Entrepreneurship is a team sport—even at the founding stage. Being connected with others is vital" (Feld and Hathaway, 2020).

Have you heard of the "PayPal Mafia?" According to Charlie Parrish's *Business Insider* article, "Meet the PayPal Mafia, the Richest Group of Men in Silicon Valley," PayPal employees and founders are called the PayPal Mafia because after founding PayPal, they founded multiple world-leading companies like Tesla, LinkedIn, Palantir Technologies, SpaceX, Affirm, Slide, Kiva, YouTube, Yelp, and Yammer. Peter Thiel, the former CEO of PayPal, became a billionaire after investing early in Facebook and other ventures. Before joining PayPal as a chief operating officer, Reid Hoffman tried unsuccessfully to build several companies, like Social Net. After PayPal's acquisition, Reid was called "the most connected man in Silicon Valley." It is no surprise that he co-founded LinkedIn within the same year that PayPal was acquired. Today, LinkedIn is the most extensive professional network globally (Parrish, 2014).

Elon Musk, Peter Thiel, and Reid Hoffman are billionaires, and even now they are actively founding, mentoring, and investing in startups. While they certainly have a talent for building businesses, their considerable wealth comes from their relationships.

Massive societal change can happen when you invite people of your network to join your mission. However, you cannot buy a network. It must be built with communication and charisma, and nobody can do it for you. The spark to build a network starts with you and its level of effectiveness depends on what, how, and why you communicate your goals to others. Robust networks get formed with a bottom-up approach and are self-sustaining. If you want your network to be active and engaged, everyone has to feel part of it. To have such an environment, you (i.e., the network's creator) must have the right mindset to make this network worthwhile.

The following chapters are about seven mindset principles to follow, create, join, or leverage the power of networks. This book is specifically targeting how individuals should behave and think to thrive in today's fast-changing world. In reality, building networks is a soft skill. This book is only scratching the surface of this superpower.

In 2022, as our economy is moving toward a startup and multistakeholder economy (see Chapters 1 and 2), the demand for entrepreneurial skills is high. We not only need them to build entirely new companies but also to build new businesses inside corporations—intrapreneurship.

IT STARTS BY BEING SELF-AWARE; ARE YOU THE OPERATING TALENT?

Susan Windham-Bannister is a business leader and world-renowned expert in open innovation and innovation ecosystem. She consults companies in strategy, market access, and healthcare policy analysis. She was named one of the ten most influential women in biotech by *The Boston Globe* in 2013 (Kirsner, 2013) and is the first African American woman in the US to lead a one-billion-dollar investment fund for Life Science.

Sue and I worked together on a few projects over the last few years. She also gave me many mentorship sessions and provided me with career advice. I interviewed her about today's startup economy and the skills needed to thrive in this new world to create change and build impactful businesses.

Before we jump into the specific skills, she mentioned, overall, a startup or any new business requires the presence of *operating talents*, which Sue defines as "the talent to build and run a company." They are the few individuals who can raise capital, inspire and hire talents, attract partners for collaborations to grow the company, and more—the people who understand business operations. For instance, operating talents would help the team go from science and clinical trials to commercialization in the pharma world. This person assists the company to go big and having a real impact. For a tech company, it would be the person who goes out, raise funds, attracts the needed talent, and builds a culture on which a company can grow and thrive.

As mentioned in Chapter 1, the startup economy is on the rise. On top of that, this new economy uses a long-term multistakeholder business model, which means that partnerships are always involved at every stage of business creation. Reid Hoffman talks about the importance of both the company's and the people's networks in his keynote address at the 2011 Endeavor Entrepreneur Summit. When building a new company or business, heading toward an unknown and uncertain destination alone is generally a recipe for failure. The key is to assemble a network to make something more likely to succeed. "That network helps you get intelligence, enables you to get the right resources, and drive forward" (Stanford eCorner, 2011).

BUILD A NETWORK TO MAGNIFY YOUR COMPANY

LinkedIn is the product of Reid's ingenuity, but it was shaped by Reid's network: co-founders, early employees, investors, customers. Reid's robust network around his company is what made the product reach almost a billion lives.

Hence, you would need to build collaboration to:

- form your team,
- attract advisors,
- get mentors,
- validate your idea with your potential customers,
- get funding,
- receive a patent,
- access new markets,
- scale,
- gain access to distribution channels,
- and so on.

Many points are not listed here, but the message is that you will need to work with many stakeholders to bring an idea to life. If you decide to be a change-maker, don't play it small. Why should people stop once they succeed to impact a thousand lives? Let's make a difference in a billion lives—why not? As Nelson Mandela said, "There is no passion to be found playing small in settling for a life that is less than the one you are capable of living." (Goodreads, 2022). It is sad if your creative idea never goes outside your village or city. The world needs it. To create real change in our world, what matters is your idea's scalability, and this can only happen through dozens, hundreds, thousands of collaborations.

Before forming thousands of them, the first step is to self-check. Are you self-aware? Are you the operating talent? Do you want to, and can you, become one? Or are you the creator of the idea and want to stay quiet? If you do not have the skills to run a business and constantly build networks, you need to find someone who does.

I am an extrovert and talk to anyone, but I know this is not the case for everyone. In a conversation with Steve Wozniak—the co-founder of Apple, very often called "Woz"—he told me and other students in a live Zoom call, "I wanted to be an engineer for life and avoid all the visibility and politics of big organizations. I am an introvert who wants to create" (Wozniak, 2021). Steve Wozniak was the engineer behind Apple's success; Steve Jobs was the operating talent. Woz wasn't the operating talent; he admits he was *simply* the technical guy. It was the combination of both skills that made Apple successful.

Susan explained that investors pay careful attention to the presence of these operating talents. If they cannot see someone in the team capable of growing the company, they are usually not interested. Why? Because all investors are looking for exits; either the company goes for sale later (acquisition), goes on the public market (IPO), or becomes a larger company. This is also why venture capital investors may request the company relocate to find more of these operating talents. Those talents are often located in innovation hotspots such as Silicon Valley, Boston, New York (in the US), London, Berlin, Paris, or Stockholm (in EU and UK).

In the end, it benefits everyone. By having the ability to scale a company, you impact more lives, and many more will come to you and invest in your idea by connecting with the vision.

Back to the initial question, what is the essential skill to build a network yourself? Sue said in a matter of milliseconds, "Telling good stories."

STORYTELLING

When I was in Silicon Valley in 2019-2020, I attended several events related to storytelling, such as Startup Grind 2020. Another one was Science through Story at UC Berkeley with Sara ElShafie, an expert storyteller who collaborates with Pixar Studio for her workshops. Another memorable event featured the trained and established storyteller Michael Margolis at the NASDAQ Entrepreneurial Center in San Francisco. He presented the research for his book, *Story 10x: Turn the Impossible into the Inevitable*, wherein he highlights, "If data is king, then context and emotion are queens."

Why do stories matter so much in business? Susan explained a story conveys the vision with conviction and goals. It helps explain how a person sees it working, what they're trying to do, what they need, and what support they require to bring the vision to life. As she pointed out, "Stories explain the why and how people can contribute." Good stories share what the present looks like, what the future can be, and how you see that vision unfolding from the beginning to the end so people can see what you hope will ultimately happen.

People want to be inspired and motivated to do something. Good stories help to accomplish this. Susan emphasized good stories include personal experiences and show data points to convince people to change. They also show how people can fit in. "Good stories are critical for developing the networks that will be formed around those ideas."

When I interviewed her, Susan was on the board of directors of Bioscience Los Angeles. She said they used the power of storytelling to partner with a VC firm, WaveMaker 360, to fund medical technology and medical devices. Susan gave a presentation and showed examples, the startups there, case studies, and the steps of the evolution of Bioscience LA. The investors were impressed by the presentation and finally agreed to invest with Bioscience LA.

Stories generate attention, get traction, attract talents and investment. They build networks.

People with an entrepreneurial mindset are ones with a DO-IT-YOURSELF attitude. How can you be one of them? The autopilot working style is alive; ninety-six percent of people in the UK admit to making most decisions on autopilot mode (Razzetti, 2018). People make decisions without clear intentions, and sometimes, it is not rational. As explained in Chapter 1, this goes back to how we grew up; we've been educated for the industrial age where teachers asked us to not take decisions but simply follow the rules and listen to their instructions.

We're currently in a hybrid world—a mix of the industrial age and the information and knowledge economy. Our new world is fast-changing, unpredictable, and uncertain from one day to the next, and it requires us to use the behavior that worked well in the past and combine it with a mindset that works very well right now: taking risks.

BECOME A MODERN HYBRID WORKER, HAVE TWO MUSCLES: DISCIPLINE AND RISK-TAKING

Diana Joseph has a PhD in leading science from Northwestern University in Illinois. She worked at Adobe in California as a learning strategist for more than six years and then worked at Citrix as Director for Innovation Enablement. Now she is an innovation consultant in Silicon Valley and CEO of the Corporate Accelerator Forum, an open innovation hub bringing corporates together to discuss best practices, cases, and relationships to unlock startup-corporation open innovation.

I interviewed Diana, and she had the following to say about the modern hybrid worker:

"I believe everybody has to be more entrepreneurial; that idea of agency and self-determination comes together with how dynamic and kind of chaotic our modern world is; being entrepreneurial means building two important muscles. One of those muscles has to do with discipline, finishing things,

checking boxes. It is being compliant, being aligned. Those who were good at school are good at this."

I need to improve that first muscle. I am someone who really likes to challenge things, and sometimes I lack empathy with the old generation and the ones following rules and processes I disagree with. We all know that in most of the world, the older generation is not programmed for taking risks. For instance, if they cannot be sure about the outcome of a certain project, they would just not do it. I like to try it out and see; experiment, even if it requires a lot of effort! Although taking risks may be suitable for an innovative project, we still interact with big companies running on the old paradigm and trying to make everything predictable. Tomorrow is about a mix of what we used to do and in the past and building the second muscle.

Diana had this to say:

"The other muscle is about risk-taking and innovation. Often, this muscle is one of the people who were not good at school. Taking the initiative versus discipline helps us do something we're not sure we know how to do and helps us survive awkwardness. It helps us be resilient in the face of failure. It helps us make a mistake and turn it into a lesson."

Most of today's workforce has the first muscle, but too many lack the second one. Around 67 percent of American employees can cite at least one reason that stopped them from taking a risk at work (Haudan, 2016).

One of the reasons we move away from collaborating is the pain we experience when working with people from different cultures. Nevertheless, collaboration and convincing people to have a different opinion is vital to creating meaningful change.

Let's move on to the importance of another skill: persuasion.

BOTTOM-UP CHANGE THROUGH THE POWER OF PER-SUASION AND NETWORKS

The iPhone has completely changed our society, and its story is fascinating. Did you know that Steve Jobs didn't want to make a phone? (Grant, 2021)

I assume we all know who Steve Jobs was. What about all the collaborators that brought this idea to life? The people who worked with Steve Jobs are one of the reasons why Steve—and Apple—were so successful. The excellent talents working with him were able to bend his reality and persuade him with new ideas.

For years, he insisted he would never make a phone. In 2005 he said, "The problem with a phone is that we're not very good going through orifices [carriers like Orange, T-Mobile, or AT&T] to get to the end-users" (Merchant, 2017). At that time, Jobs believed the network providers would have too much power over the consumer, deciding who could access their network or not. Jobs thought it would be too hard to collaborate with them and interact with the consumers directly. His team persuaded him he should do it, and Jobs finally agreed.

Later, he didn't want any outside apps. It took another year
for him to reconsider this. Finally, the firm launched the
App Store in 2007. Within nine months after the launch, the
Apple Store experienced a billion downloads, and a decade
later, the iPhone had generated more than one trillion dollars
in revenue.

Laura Ceci and Jon Erlichman reported that Apple's App
Store revenue since its inception is staggering.

2009: $769 million
2010: $2 billion
2011: $3 billion
2012: $5 billion
2013: $10 billion
2014: $15 billion
2015: $20 billion
2016: $29 billion
2017: $39 billion
2018: $47 billion
2019: $56 billion
2020: $72 billion

According to the research of Adam Grant, an organizational
psychologist at Wharton University, most of the time, people in power are not listening. We all know leaders who are
overconfident and stubborn. "When someone tried hard to
alter their thinking, they snapped back like a rubber band"
(Grant, 2021). Our jobs as aspiring change-makers are not to
stop being creative if someone says no. We have to learn to
join forces with others and persuade that person.

Steve Jobs was confident in his thinking, but he invited people to challenge and help him overcome his own worst instincts. People like Tony Fadell were one of them. Tony is the inventor of the iPod and a co-creator of the iPhone. He worked for months with his engineering team to change Steve's objections and build networks around him to make his idea possible. Tony is a *master persuader* and used the power of networks—him and his team—to change and influence Steve's mind. This shaped the story of the Apple we know today.

To sum this up, having an idea is great, but if nobody listens to it, the idea will never take off the ground. The chapter reminded me how important it is to think about scaling to produce and change something meaningful in this world. Your relationships are everything, and your network will magnify your company and product.

TAKE ACTION:

DO-IT-YOURSELF and do the work to build the network. There is no magic pill!

It starts with self-awareness. Who are you? The engineer or the operating talent? If you want to lead the change, learn how to run a business, understand business operations, and take storytelling classes. If you're an engineer, hire talent that complements your skills.

Build the two muscles: discipline and taking risks, and adopting an entrepreneurial mindset.

Join Toastmasters International to practice public speaking, improve communication, and build leadership skills.

Get convinced by the power of storytelling: read scientific journal articles such as Sara ElShafie's, Making Science Meaningful for Broad Audiences Through Stories, or the 2010 PNAS journal article, "Speaker-Listener Neural Coupling Underlies Successful Communication," by Greg J. Stephens, Lauren J. Silbert, and Uri Hasson.

Take online storytelling classes such as The Art of Storytelling available at Khan Academy (a course made by Pixar Studios).

Read Michael Margolis' book, Story 10x: Turn the Impossible into the Inevitable and learn storytelling for the business world.

Learn persuasion. My favorite book about this is Never Split the Difference: Negotiating as If Your Life Depended on It by Chris Voss with Tahl Raz.

CHAPTER 5

Principle 2: Blow Up Your Borders

---

*"The mind, once stretched by a new idea,
never returns to its original dimensions."*

—RALPH WALDO EMERSON

At the time of writing this, only 13 percent of the US workforce is passionate about and highly engaged with their jobs (Hagel et al., 2017). In Germany, it is only about 15 percent (Nink, 2015). This is a disaster. An unengaged workforce affects our society, businesses, and everyone. In a survey of thirty million employees, it was found that companies with a highly engaged workforce outperformed their peers by 147 percent in earnings per share (Sorenson, 2013). Additionally, engaged employees are 27 percent more likely to report excellent performance (Witters and Agrawal, 2015). Those studies and data explain that you need to be passionate, engaged, and working in a field where you can use your strengths to deliver extraordinary results.

Steve Jobs mentioned in his Stanford commencement address of 2005:

"Your work is going to fill a large part of your life, and the only way to be truly satisfied is to do what you believe is great work. And the only way to do great work is to love what you do. If you haven't found it yet, keep looking. Don't settle."

He said it for a reason. Changing the world requires a lot of passion because this passion will help you stand up when something in life puts you down. One of the ways to thrive, create solutions, and change the world is to build networks by blowing up imaginary societal borders.

This problem starts with how we've been raised at home and how we evolve as a society. When we are young, we try to find what we want to do in life. Then, when we're about seventeen to twenty years old, we realize there's so much social expectation, and we start to go with the flow of the proverbial river, just like everyone else.

To create new connections in a network, you first need to know that these relationships can be made. A strong network starts with self-awareness, passion, and curiosity to connect with others.

THE PATH TO SELF-DISCOVERY

I am French-German and grew up in France. In France, ambitious individuals aim for the renowned engineer title (not considered a job, but a title). In France, being an engineer is much more than mechanical and electrical engineering;

it can refer to environmental science, the textile industry, pure organic chemistry, or informatics. In France, it's the most renowned title you can get. The Ph.D. qualification is not essential; it's a plus, but nobody cares. It's different in Germany, where becoming an engineer is less recognized. In Germany, ambitious people want to get their Ph.D. qualifications. There, it's everything. If you go to India, everyone wants to work for the government or become an engineer (mechanical or electrical). And so, depending on the country, everything will change, and social expectations will change.

Therefore, it is hard to do what we love because we unconsciously want to fulfill these societal expectations. In her TEDx talk, "The Psychology of Career Decision," Sharon Belden highlights that "throughout much of human history, people didn't choose a line of work. You did what your parents did. What you did for a living was prescribed from where you were from, your gender, and your social class." This is what I experienced in my own life and see again and again in my friends' families. We are usually pushed to follow the path of our parents. When our parents try to guide us, they typically tell us what they've done or were told to do, without necessarily trying to understand what drives us to do what we are passionate about.

As Steve Jobs said, "love what you do," and I am unaware of any entrepreneur who will not advise you to work on what you're passionate about. But how do we do this when we get so much pressure from the external world? Most people I know are not aware of their passion and strengths, mainly because they didn't try enough different things, and now the older they get, the more they are afraid to try new things because of fear.

I chatted with Lauren Brown, a friend who recently relocated from the US to France to join a company as a training specialist.

"The big issue I was having was collaborating. I was asking myself, why am I so stressed about getting a 'no' from my boss? I reflected on this internally; what is my fear? If I'm completely transparent, it's because of job security. I'm a foreigner living in France, and I'm on a trial period."

Lauren's situation is something I have seen many times. We all escape fear and seek security, and I believe our school system doesn't help. We were not allowed to ask for different things; we needed to follow the rules like everybody else. I think one of the ways to find what we are truly passionate about is to take time for ourselves, and sometimes this means taking a step back.

When I was writing my bachelor's thesis, I asked my supervisor, "When do you think is a good time to take a break and travel; pause and reflect on life?" He answered, "You can't do a break now. First, finish your studies; get your master's degree." But when I asked other people the same question, I received different answers, like, "First, get your first job," or "First, get your three years of experience." I concluded there is no perfect time; it is different for everyone, and nobody can schedule it for you. You have to make a decision based on your aspirations and your goals. You have to redefine these constantly.

In my case, I was fortunate. I was able to take a break from the timeline of social expectations and travel. I studied chemistry in Germany, and many students I knew took a six-month or twelve-month break before, during, or after their studies. They inspired me to do the same. In Germany, while staying enrolled, I was allowed to "press pause" and come back later. This is unique, and you can't do it in France or probably many other countries either.

So, I took several breaks. In total, I traveled for over twelve months and visited over thirty-five countries. I started with my first significant international experience when I was eighteen. My English was terrible, and I went to a UK university to do an intensive four-week course. I landed in a class with twenty-six internal Chinese students and two Russians.

Figure 5.1: The younger me (eighteen years old) with some of my Chinese classmates from my time in the United Kingdom, one of the first times I discovered the incredible power of an international environment.

Being in all those different environments made me understand the big picture. Traveling across eight countries in Africa helped me realize the importance of communities and rituals that connect and bond them. In 2018, I went to Mexico for a research internship at the University of Puebla. I saw how scientists did experiments with nearly no infrastructure. They used tubes they bought at the repair shop to create inert conditions, whereas, in Germany, we used the latest state-of-the-art equipment to do the same. They inspired me by being okay with chaos and still producing outstanding results and publishing in international journals such as the *Journal of the American Chemical Society* (JACS).

Moving outside your silos helps you to understand yourself and others. I realized people's behavior depended on where they came from and how they were raised. Trying different things help us discover what we are genuinely passionate about, our strengths, and what we love. It's the path to self-discovery, which is the foundation of our careers! Not only that, but it also helps us to remove our confirmation bias and increase our creativity.

REMOVE CONFIRMATION BIAS AND ENHANCE CREATIVITY

I wanted to understand if this was something others experienced as well. I had the chance to interview Mark Koester. Mark grew up in Omaha, Nebraska, and went to DePaul University in Chicago to study philosophy. He later did his graduate studies in Paris and Strasbourg, France. Upon completion, he moved to China, where he spent nearly a decade, among other things, living as a digital nomad in a mountain town in western Sichuan. When it comes to experiencing different environments, he was the person I had to talk to!

Mark did more than just travel; he co-founded Startup Weekend, a three-day innovation competition attracting aspiring entrepreneurs who want to experience startup life. Mark organized it hundreds of times between 2014 and 2018 in various cities in China and other Asian countries. In 2015, Startup Weekend was acquired by Techstars. As of 2021, Techstars has operated the three-day event in over 150 countries with more than 428,000 participants (Techstars, 2021). Today, Mark is on a mission to make a self-tracking and data-driven life a reality. He tracks everything (health data, Zoom calls, music, etc.) using monitoring devices and computing power leveraging AI to help people become more self-aware, make better decisions, and perform better in their lives.

I asked Mark how his perspective on life changed when he worked and lived in many different environments. He confirmed it helped to remove confirmation bias. "It's probably the strongest force in the universe." Today, Mark tries to challenge himself, instead of automatically agreeing with his assumptions. He added there are always assumptions to be tested in every product, and the step of testing those assumptions shouldn't be overlooked. Being abroad and blowing up borders removes your confirmation bias and helps you be more creative.

In a study led by William Maddux, the aim was to test if there was a link between living abroad and creativity (Maddux, 2009). In five studies employing a multimethod approach using American and European students, the results were as follows:

- Studies 1 and 2 provided initial demonstrations that time spent living abroad (but not time spent traveling abroad) showed a positive relationship with creativity.
- Study 3 demonstrated that priming foreign living experiences temporarily enhanced creative tendencies for participants who had previously lived abroad.
- Study 4 showed the degree to which individuals had adapted to different cultures while living abroad and how it boosted creativity.
- Study 5 found that priming the experience of adapting to a foreign culture temporarily enhanced creativity for participants who had previously lived abroad.

In a world where resilience is everything, crossing and blowing up borders can boost our self-confidence and make us better leaders and human beings.

REDUCE FEAR AND TAKE BETTER DECISIONS

Vas Narasimhan, CEO of Novartis, one of the largest pharmaceutical companies in the world, supports the importance of experimenting with different positions in different departments:

"Don't underestimate the importance of getting multidisciplinary exposure. Most people get worried when they have to make those jumps. I've had a career at Novartis where I've worked in commercial areas and marketing areas—so most of my time in R&D worked across four different areas of the

business—and so with that diversity of experiences it enables you to make the right decisions" (Narasimhan et al., 2021).

Changing roles to see the big picture can help us discover where we perform best. Doing so is not just a "nice to have" but will soon be a "must-have." Many of us will be forced to—in the next decade, over one hundred million workers may need to switch occupations (Meakin, 2021).

Compared to our parents' generation, moving outside our silos and trying different jobs across various departments in other countries and companies can be advantageous. Additionally, we make connections between all these experiences and build networks. In our startup and multistakeholder economy, these networks are the power of our time as they give us access to knowledge and ideas, resources such as capital and infrastructure, and the right people to join your mission. Having that as an asset helps make successful collaborations and partnerships with others.

Having that multidisciplinary exposure helps you to be confident and reduce fear.

Lauren, my friend mentioned earlier who moved from the US to France, shared she felt trapped in her work and didn't feel she had other options. She was afraid of asking her boss questions like, "Can I receive marketing training?" She didn't want to hear no. Together, we brainstormed about the idea of being resourceful and asking for advice from other people in the same industry, which is what she did. They told her she had nothing to worry about; they explained that if something went wrong, other options were available.

"I realized we have to network all the time, not only when we need something. We need to connect with and help others regularly. When you have this networking mindset, you do not feel limited anymore; you know other options are available. Later on, I gained confidence, and I started to ask my boss about the training I wanted to have to perform better at my job."

When we talk and network with people outside our discipline, we feel empowered. Why? Because it expands our *cognitive map*. Edward Tolman discussed that humans and other animals have a "cognitive map" that allows them to navigate their everyday spatial environments (Tolman, 1948). Research shows that being in new locations impacts how our brains work (Houston, 2016). So, moving to a new environment will fire you up as different neurons in your brain fire, which helps you stay agile, competitive, and fearless.

By applying other people's thoughts and guidance, Lauren could ask questions confidently. Later on, her boss offered her many options for training to grow and progress in the company. In the end, Lauren was able to be more collaborative inside the company because she regularly networked with people outside.

The lesson is this: Many obstacles will come in our way, stopping us from doing what we truly want. One of them is the fear of getting a "NO." Here the same applies. By experimenting with many different things, we will connect with so many organizations and people, learn what others do, and motivate them.

Crossing and blowing up borders is not only essential for finding our true calling and being confident, but it is also necessary for thriving in today's fast-changing world. Due to the rise of exponential technologies, mixed disciplines, and interconnected societies, focusing on one niche business makes us vulnerable and inflexible in today's world. The solution is to work with an interdisciplinary team. Each team member would represent a different place and therefore help everyone in the team build networks.

MULTIDISCIPLINARY TEAMS WITH COMPLEMENTARY SKILLS WILL WIN

As a reminder, we know traditional companies want uniformity and control. I see this firsthand with my current employer. It is a Japanese company with Japanese culture—using hierarchies and group decision-making processes known as *nemawashi* and the *ringi* system. However, it is tough for new employees with a pure US or European way of working to do things differently.

Entrepreneurs and startups operate in, and benefit from, the opposite way of work. It is well known that monocultures and groupthink are deadly for startups. To have the right environment to cultivate change, we need more diversity.

Therefore, make sure to work for and hire the right people to have a multidisciplinary team.

CONCLUSION

This chapter highlighted the importance of building an extensive, diverse network of experiences and people by blowing up self-made, imaginary borders. We need to forget the old rules from our parent's generation regarding careers, and we should trust ourselves to take the leap and try new things. That means blowing them up—the border of your country (getting experience abroad), the imaginary boundary of the team inside your organization, or the border of your field of expertise.

We need to help more people to discover their strengths and passion, and many need to be more self-aware. Once the passion is ignited, curiosity follows. Today, having worked in, and traveled to, over thirty-five countries, I feel I know myself, which will help me progress in my career. In terms of innovation and creativity, studies have proven that being abroad makes people more creative. Mark, a serial entrepreneur, insists a network of people can help us remove confirmation bias. For example, a diverse network is better at testing assumptions in product building. The idea of changing departments across the company helped Vas, the CEO of Novartis, to make better decisions and become the empathetic leader he is today. Networking with people outside Lauren's team enabled her to feel limitless and confident.

As you can imagine, the insights we get from the network of person A and the network we get from person B are not equal. To build robust networks, we must understand the power of cognitive diversity, and our networks must be as diverse as possible. Over time, the network gets more powerful and can make an idea or decision making less fragile. Hence, it will enable you to understand others, build a holistic view of a problem, and help you to tap into an infinite source of inspiration. The more you blow up your borders and the more you network with the right people, the more you feel capable to change the world positively.

TAKE ACTION:

Take online classes and learn a new field on platforms such as Coursera, Udemy, or LinkedIn Learning. This is a great way to expand your horizons. Speak to someone who inspires you to get guidance on what skills you need to learn.

Travel, study, or work abroad to expand your awareness and find your passion. It is also a way to understand new cultures. An excellent way to do this is through an exchange program or to volunteer with a service like workaway.info. There is no age limit, and it transforms people's lives.

If you're an employee, ask your manager if you could try a different position. If the answer is no, ask why and how you could potentially make it happen. If you're convinced you want to try, explore outside your organization.

If you want to change the company and move into a new role, apply for internships. A friend of mine applied for an internship and switched from lab work to business in a matter of months. Internships are way easier to get.

Alternatively, use your network to get hired by someone you know who is willing to teach you.

Join diverse teams or, if you can employ people with various skills, hire people with diverse skills. It is incredible to learn from colleagues who are different from you.

Ask questions all the time. Why? How? What is the background of this choice? Be extremely curious. Consider how your confirmation bias is evolving.

CHAPTER 6

Principle 3: Be of Value; Give before You Get

How may I serve?

What if, before starting all your discussions, you would ask yourself this question: *How may I serve?*

This is my favorite principle of the book. I have seen way too many people focus on transactions in the business world instead of building relationships. What is the difference between a giver and a taker? As Adam Grants put it in his article, "In the Company of Givers and Takers," "When they act like givers, they contribute to others without seeking anything in return. They might offer assistance, share knowledge, or make valuable introductions. When they act like takers, they try to get other people to serve their ends while carefully guarding their own expertise and time."

Usually, people ask themselves unconsciously, "What is in it for me?" Or, as an acquaintance mentioned to me, "The hard part is where to focus, how to make sure my giving is creating an impact, how to deal with people who only take and never give." This person is correct; as of today, only a quarter of the workforce are givers (Grant, 2013), making it very hard to give when most people aren't.

It is straightforward; when people only give something to others when they are sure they will get something in return, they behave selfishly. If we know we can be helpful and don't do it because they think this person is a taker, then we don't change the more significant systemic problem: Everyone is focused on themselves. In the multistakeholder economy we live in today, more people should go from *ego* to *echo* and move away from being focused on themselves, start focusing on the networks that share the same intentions. We should be focusing on building relationships.

A meta-analysis from the University of Arizona, led by Nathan Podsakoff, investigated thirty-eight organizational behavior studies, representing more than 3,500 business units from different industries. They found a robust correlation between employee giving and desirable business outcomes. Giving predicts a unit's increase in productivity, higher profitability, efficiency, and customer satisfaction, along with lower costs and turnover rates. As mentioned in the *Harvard Business Review* article, "In the Company of Givers" by Curt Nickisch, "Generosity can be guided in the direction of greatest impact."

When people have a giving mindset and try to be of value, everyone benefits from it. This chapter will explore why it is even more relevant now—in today's fast-changing society—to be a giver.

WE ARE DEPENDENT ON OTHERS

Let me first emphasize why giving is even more important in the twenty-first century. Today, *you are not alone*. As mentioned in the first three chapters of this book, entrepreneurs will drive our economy, and companies will need to have more entrepreneurial talents inside of theirs. Every organization must collaborate with different stakeholders (other companies, startups, NGOs, the government, and more) to innovate, generate new businesses, and solve problems.

Today and tomorrow's economy is ecosystem driven with multiple stakeholders. This means our economy relies predominantly on relationships and networks. Startup founders know it; they depend on their ability to detect, identify, and effectively use the resources available to them, such as mentorship, large corporations, PR, media, or simply financial capital.

As Brad Feld and Ian Hathaway mention in their book, *The Startup Community Way: Evolving an Entrepreneurial Ecosystem*, a thriving innovation ecosystem happens when all players are here and help the most critical piece of the puzzle: the entrepreneurs. In the book, you will find a diagram representing what Silicon Valley is doing (see Figure 6.1).

Entrepreneurs are in the middle. Around them at the first level, you have human capital, intellectual capital, financial capital, institutional capital, physical capital. All of that is called "cultural and network capital."

At the second level, you find all of the other essentials that make an entrepreneur successful. Accelerators, incubators & co-working, other entrepreneurial support organizations, large corporations, media, research and advocacy groups, government (local/regional), government (national), universities, service providers, investors, coaches, advisors, mentors, startups employees, serial entrepreneurs.

Actors and Factors in an Entrepreneurial Ecosystem

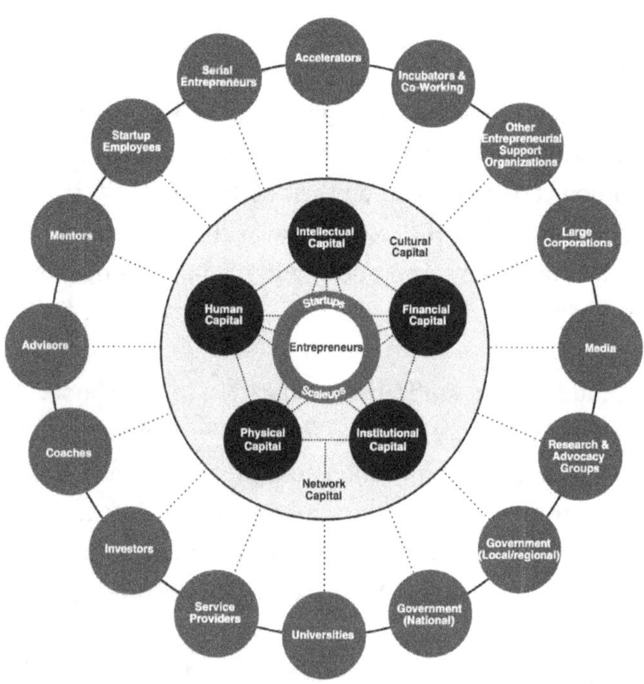

Figure 6.1: Graphic featuring the wide networks surrounding an entrepreneur. The entrepreneur's ability to tap into this network will determine how successful he/she can be. (Feld and Hathaway, 2020)

We live in a time when our economy relies on startups and collaboration. I have heard so many times the only thing entrepreneurs need is financial capital. This isn't true. First, capital comes in various forms: intellectual, economic, institutional, physical, and human. Second, the entrepreneurs will need to connect with countless stakeholders to scale their idea. How often do we see people trying to do things by themselves? This can't work anymore.

It's incredible to realize—in 2022 and beyond—how dependent we are on each other to gain a competitive advantage. To have better and easier access to these essential stakeholders, one has to build an authentic and respected brand. And a critical part of building this brand is to make an incredible first impression. This happens when we provide value first and help others along the way. By creating a reputation for being that helpful person, more people will be willing to make introductions.

Building networks is a superpower, and when we find a way to value others, we accelerate the rate at which we develop that superpower.

We cannot just ask for help to collaborate with the ecosystem. We need to give first. Brad Feld is a co-founder of the Foundry Group (a venture capital firm) and has been an early-stage investor and entrepreneur since 1987. He previously co-founded Mobius Venture Capital and Techstars, a seed startup accelerator, and before that, Intensity Ventures. Brad was an early investor in Harmonix, Zynga, MakerBot, and Fitbit.

Brad is the person who promoted the *#GiveFirst* principle. He wrote, mandated, and even made it part of the code of conduct of Techstars. This is how he defines it, along with Techstars co-founder David Cohen: "In the startup world, *Give First* means simply trying to help anyone—especially entrepreneurs—with no expectation of getting anything back. It's the pay-it-forward principle that builds strong startup networks" (Cohen and Feld, 2022).

In the code of conduct of Techstars (Techstars, 2021), you can find seven principles for the *#GiveFirst* mindset:

1. We help others whenever possible. We are all busy, but when the ask is sincere and realistic, we respond and help. We respect each other's time and are clear and focused on our requests.
2. We respond quickly in network. We make every attempt to prioritize and respond to requests from fellow Techstars network members, ideally within two business days.
3. We deliberately create a virtuous cycle. We proactively work to give back to the ecosystem by giving first to others in our community with no specific expectations of return.
4. We appreciate the help of others. No one does it alone; startups are a team activity. We express our appreciation for the help of our customers, mentors, and others that make our success possible.

5. We respect "no" as an answer. If another member says no to a request, we respect their decision.

6. We share talent and business opportunities. Whenever we have finalist candidates whom we choose not to hire directly, we share them with others in the network. When we become aware of good business opportunities that we choose not to pursue directly, we share them with others in the network.

7. We are committed to building a safe, sustainable, long-lasting, and prosperous global society through our business activities. We believe in solving environmental issues, such as climate change, to contribute to building a people- and planet-friendly future.

Brad is not the only one promoting the Give Before You Get mindset principle. Let's continue to learn from successful individuals about how giving and serving others, without expectations in return, has helped them.

THE BUSIEST AND MOST SUCCESSFUL PEOPLE FIND TIME TO GIVE

Nina Luu is an investor and serial founder. I met her in San Francisco at a pitch event featuring tech startups. After the conference, I followed up with her and requested a meeting. We spoke about entrepreneurship and venture capital during our session and how I could be the leader I was hoping to become. A year later, everything shut down due to COVID-19, and I had to go back to Europe. It was a culture shock, coming back to my hometown with no startup culture and few opportunities in terms of job growth.

I reached out to Nina and asked for some advice. I was ecstatic when she agreed to mentor me every week throughout 2020. I was lucky she had time during the pandemic because I was totally at a loss for finding a job and didn't know how to make money. I was fortunate I had some savings and could move back home to my parents. Nina saw I had potential but needed a plan of execution. During the first few sessions, Nina listened and learned about my strengths and weaknesses. Based on that, we developed a plan with achievable goals. With much resistance on my side, Nina pushed me to set very high goals—dream goals—such as a financial target of six figures that was way beyond what I could conceive. We also talked about my dream job: becoming a CEO of a multinational company. At first, I was uncomfortable with these big goals, but Nina said, "If you don't feel it, you won't be able to achieve it."

It took a while, but with her encouragement and consistently pointing out my strengths and abilities, I felt confident the goals we set out were achievable. Once my confidence kicked in, I got my dream job within three months of her mentorship. The only thing Nina asked of me was to pay it forward when another person needed my help. The biggest lesson I have taken away from many conversations with Nina is the power of giving.

I asked Nina what giving means for her. For her, giving applies to all aspects of life. "It's how I live my life, whether it is giving to my daughter or a business transaction. It's *everything*." Nina mentioned even her father had this giving mindset; he lived his life asking every morning, "How may I serve?" This is now how Nina approaches all interactions:

to be of service to others. Her father always told her the best giving is anonymous and had no expectations of receiving anything back. Trust that when you need something, it will show up and not necessarily from the person you helped.

I often wonder why people do not give. I asked Nina, and she said, "Sometimes they haven't been taught to give, or sometimes they are in a situation where they need to take. It is okay to take when you are in need. If you are not wired to give, try it and see the benefits."

It doesn't matter whether you benefit from giving or not. It comes back to how you define success, and what motivates you to do your work. As Nina puts it, "No matter what you do, it has to make a difference in the lives of others." You give to see a different world. Nina explained there are problems in society she cannot solve independently. She had struggled in venture capital as there were few women in VC. She hopes to invest in more women- and multicultural-led businesses (such as people of color), also called for women and minority-owned businesses (WMBEs). She mentioned this is one of the reasons she helps young people—because they are the future.

In fact, only 1.4 percent of more than eighty two trillion dollars of US-based assets are entrusted to diverse-owned firms. What does this mean? It means from the eighty-two trillion dollars being invested in mutual funds, hedge funds, private equity funds, and real estate funds, investors only entrust 1.4 percent of assets are owned by women and/or people of color. (Knight Foundation, 2021).

Sometimes you don't give for yourself; you give because you identified a more significant societal problem, and you hope more people will act to solve it because they received your help. You do not try to do it for your benefit; you try to benefit the network, the larger ecosystem.

At the end of one of our conversations, I had learned giving even affects our well-being. Nina said, "Giving helps me to make a positive impact, and this motivates me." Giving also improves your health and work productivity. She added, "Success is about relationships, your health, the equation of everything. It's about the balance." Having poor relationships with your family and others make you stressed out, which affects your work.

Like Nina, other investors worldwide have noticed the same about the art of giving and sharing in Silicon Valley. Carsten Jens Maschmeyer is a German billionaire businessman, investor, and panel member of the German investment television series Die Höhle der Löwen ("The Lions' Den"). In November 2021, he posted on LinkedIn about his startup tour in San Francisco. He mentioned four things the place does differently from Germany:

1. The deals are faster.
2. The pitches are focused on growth and vision rather than cost reduction and slow growth.
3. Startups fight hard to get more people (their motto is, "You are whom you hire!"). In Germany, on the other hand, many people think good people are too expensive.
4. Last but not least, networking is everything. VC funds like to share their deal flow (i.e., they give first) and see

where they can invest with other investors. Founders of various startups also help each other with recruiting, customer acquisition, and contacts (Maschmeyer, 2021).

People focus on giving in this ecosystem, which is the most vibrant innovation ecosystem globally. This is not only relevant to receiving funding or funding the best startups. Giving helps you to get jobs and accelerate your career drastically.

On this topic, an acquaintance mentioned, "You have to be in a privileged position to give in the first place." In other words, you have to have something you can give away freely—time, money, knowledge. It is easy to find an excuse to not try to be of value to other people. What does "privilege" mean anyway? If you do not have money, you may have time to support people. If you have no money or time to give, maybe you have two minutes to write to someone you know that could potentially be helpful to that person? If you can't do that, what are you waking up for? It's not about helping everyone, but helping those we believe have great potential to solve a problem we try to solve too and are trustworthy. That's the least we can do.

When I was leaving San Francisco, I posted on my own LinkedIn channel how grateful I was to have had this experience, and I said thank you to all the people I had met, hoping I would stay in touch with them. The post received fifty-three comments from different people who wished me luck with the next steps. One of them was Nsikak Edet, a Nigerian web developer, who commented:

"Well, it's been months since we last had a chat. Just wanted you to know that before I messaged you last year on career advice as a young chemistry graduate, I had earlier messaged tons of people. You were the only one who replied. That gave me hope. And made me feel part of a global community. A feeling you don't usually get from being a Nigerian. Wishing you better days ahead."

When I helped him and said yes to having a chat, I was a student with no money and no significant business relationships to offer him. However, I took the time to reply. This shows that giving is a value, it is a state of being we do for a lifetime and receiving messages like the one above is the reward.

Sometimes, when we are of value, we get more, such as job positions. Up to 85 percent of jobs are filled via networking (Turczynski, 2021). In my case, I *never* got a job from an online job portal. All of my positions were created through recommendations; through the relationships I created and nurtured. Through my network, I self-created. Every time I met senior executives, I tried to be of value, and as a reward, they helped me out. Some would say this is "butt-kissing," but is it? No, because when I met them the first time, I first and foremost tried to add value. It's only later I asked for a job; sometimes it was years later. To me, this is a clear distinction.

BEING OF VALUE AS AN ACCELERATOR OF YOUR CAREER

To thrive in today's fast-changing world, it is essential to build credibility and reliability. Building relationships with top management accelerates building networks and enables co-creation. So, how do you make a connection with them? Again, always focus on them, not you. Read their work, comment on it, share the stories you found about them. Usually, they will be pleased because no one else is doing it. Then, you can propose to prepare a study, a report, or a presentation for them. The key is to identify their issues and offer your help, even if they didn't ask for it. Usually, they have nothing against it if you identified a problem they are dealing with. Show the results. Every time I did that in the past, they were very impressed. They always liked the outcomes. As a result, they wanted to help me in my career as well.

Something similar happened to Keith Ferrazzi, who is recognized as a global thought leader in the relational and collaborative sciences. As chairman of Ferrazzi Greenlight (a global consulting and coaching firm in strategic relationship management) and the Greenlight Research Institute (which gathers data and insights about the future of work), he identifies behaviors that block international organizations from reaching their goals. He transforms them by coaching new behaviors that increase growth and shareholder value. He is also the author of the New York Times bestsellers, *Never Eat Alone* and *Who's Got Your Back?* His work focuses on the importance of positive relationships to business success. He also works with Tony Robbins, Peter Diamandis, and Adam Grant and give talks worldwide.

In the Mindvalley online course, Ultimate Leadership, Keith Ferrazzi mentions, "The fastest way to extend your influence is to tap into people upon you," which encapsulates well what happened to me. I tried to add value as much as I could; many doors have opened by doing so.

What is interesting is Keith comes from an impoverished social class. His father was a steelworker, and his mother was a cleaning lady. His father knew his son had to go to an excellent private school, and he found a way to convince the director of a private high school to take his son and provide him with a scholarship. His father wasn't elite, but he was bold enough to ask for help. He understood he had to tap into the people above him. Keith went on to graduate from Yale University.

Keith was less than thirty years old when he became the youngest CMO (chief marketing officer) of Deloitte US. How did he do this? He succeeded in having a great relationship with a senior executive. As a passion project, he wrote and published a report on leadership, comparing the different leadership styles of other Fortune 500 companies. The executive knew about the report and was astonished by the great work, and as a result, promoted Keith, first to partner and then CMO of the company (Mindvalley, 2022).

GIVING AS A STARTING POINT FOR TOMORROW'S LEADERSHIP

I learned about Keith and his accomplishments when I attended Mindvalley Live, a human transformation and entrepreneurship conference in Los Angeles, shortly before COVID-19 hit in 2020. After watching Keith, I took his online class, Ultimate Leadership on *Mindvalley*. In this class, he teaches one can't do anything alone in today's world, that relationships are crucial to our success.

Keith coined the term "co-elevation," defined as "an approach to collaboratively achieve new levels of success through a team's commitment to co-create and challenge each other to go higher" (Co-Elevation, 2021). As Kathy Caprino puts it in her *Forbes* article, co-elevation "is a key foundational behavior that we can all use to lead, connect, and elevate ourselves and others powerfully and effectively, even without pre-established authority."

Leadership is a daily process; it's about improving people, teams, and operations. In Keith's class, he talks about the twelve skills of a leader in the twenty-first century. The *most critical* skill? Be focused on co-creation and collaboration; serve people, and focus on a collective approach.

 Isn't it obvious? *Giving is an enabler to build networks. It will unleash this superpower!*

CONCLUSION

Research demonstrates having the intention to help and to share our own expertise with others can lead to success in today's collaborative, networked organizations. (Nickisch, 2017)

I learned early in my career that focusing on adding value right at the beginning of each conversation is the most powerful secret to being liked by others. In Silicon Valley, I learned that successful entrepreneurs, investors, and mentors all do it. Today's world is so difficult to understand and be up to date, so being strongly connected with others is even more relevant.

The one trying to give to get something in return never sustains long-lasting relationships. Doing so is a recipe for disaster. The startup and multistakeholder economy cannot work with people behaving that way. From Ego to Echo: While being egocentric makes you more distant from anyone else, acting in an "echo" manner will make room for everyone. The overall ecosystem will thrive better that way.

In this chapter, we learned a powerful way to accelerate our career and climb the ladder faster is to tap into the people around us (collaborating with top management and making them successful, even if they didn't ask for it). Brad Feld has one of the most successful startup organizations globally because all the staff and entrepreneurs are trained to *#GiveFirst*. Nina was a successful investor because she gave so much to her people. I was able to receive dream opportunities worldwide based on the relationships I built, thanks to my intention of helping. Keith was able to become the youngest CMO of Deloitte by leading up.

I hope you have begun to realize you have NOTHING to lose by helping others; you can only win. The reality is you will never achieve anything alone. Relationships are crucial for your success and your chance to create change in our society.

TAKE ACTION:

Watch Adam Grant's TEDx Talk, "Are You a Giver or a Taker?"

Listen to Brad Feld's podcast, "Give First." Watch any of his courses, available on various platforms, including LinkedIn Learning.

Suppose you want to impress your boss. Ask yourself what would your boss needs in his daily job; how can you serve? Do it without waiting for him to ask for it.

Get experience in Silicon Valley. If you can't go and live there, try to attend something remotely, join communities, participate in events. Connect with those people. Or join communities created there, like A360 from Peter Diamandis.

If you're part of an organization and you want to establish this mindset principle: Be of Value; Give Before You Get— Write a code of conduct, and share it with anyone who works with you.

Read Dale Carnegie's classic book, How to Win Friends and Influence People.

Any time you meet a person, try to be in the other person's shoes. What does he/she need? How could you be helpful? If you do not know how to help them, do you know someone in your network who can help them?

CHAPTER 7

Principle 4. Start Small, Grow Big, with Purpose

---

*"Start with small groups loosely connected
and united by a shared purpose."*

— GREG SATELL

In my experience, every time a project ended up being successful, it was when people opened the challenge to anyone who wanted to participate and got the "early adopters" in, the people who were more excited about the project than anyone else. Don't force anyone; welcome the volunteers. For that to happen, you also need to open up your tasks to others, share information about it, ask for feedback comments, and allow them to participate so it can be improved.

I have been involved in countless projects over the last ten years. Apart from studying, living, and working internationally, I have also been involved in dozens of online communities and non-profit organizations. These include my former alumni organization, TEDxSan Francisco, Lean Startup, and the MIT COVID-19 Challenge series involving thousands of participants globally.

Every single time, the teams, organizations, or companies decide how to communicate and manage projects. There is no golden rule to do it, but I have noticed that sometimes projects are open to the world and welcome everyone to participate; the team picks people, and it works organically. However, managers often choose people to run and grow a project in the corporate world. The second option usually has a higher rate of failure. Getting the best team based on the project starts by openly sharing what you do and why.

What annoys me the most is I repeatedly come across people who are unwilling to share their ideas. They are reluctant to collaborate, with an it's-my-idea attitude, afraid of losing the credit, or afraid people will know if the project fails. Today, even with new ways of communicating, like Yammer, Teams, Slack, etc., I still see people writing secure emails and not making any efforts to enhance transparency in the team.

We need more open ways to communicate. We need more transparency. We need to let people ask more questions. We need to create more collaborative and autonomous communities that are self-sustaining and self-growing. This is how change happens through networks, the power of our time.

The workforce needs more transparency and open communication, not just because young people sitting at the bottom of the ladder can benefit from it, but because it makes all employees feel part of the mission. As mentioned in the previous chapter, we need more engaged employees to solve our world's biggest problems. We don't have extra time to solve the world's biggest problems. Solutions need to be implemented faster.

THE IMPACT OF THE INTERNET ON NETWORK-DRIVEN CHANGES

Nearly the entire population of the planet could potentially be connected to the internet over the next decade or two. This impact automatically affects the speed at which companies can attract millions of users.

Jeff Desjardins' 2018 blog article, "How Long Does It Take to Hit 50 Million Users?" explains it well. It could take as long as twenty years to implement some new transformative technologies, like connected electric cars, in the market; however, in most cases, today's digital technologies can hit fifty million users very quickly. Did you know it took airlines sixty-eight years to hit fifty million users? Automobiles, fifty-two years. The internet took seven years, but Pokémon Go—nineteen days! Sure, an app can't be compared to a plane, but it still highlights the network effects. The more people are connected to the internet, the more connections exist. When there are only two users, you have one connection. When there are eight users, you have twenty-eight connections. And as a result, the adoption of an idea can be exponential.

With the rise of our digital world, the power is no longer at the top of the hierarchy but across the network. Everybody who is part of it can start to drive a change.

START WITH A SMALL GROUP

To better understand how networks work, are created, and evolve, I interviewed one of the leading experts on transformational change. I met Greg Satell through my friend Diana Joseph, with whom I hosted *The Ecosystem Show* on Clubhouse. In this show, we interview key players in the innovation ecosystem from all over the world. Greg wanted to help us grow a more extensive community to increase our impact, so he invited us to host the show at his Clubhouse Club, *Change Agents.* When I looked into who he was, I realized Greg was very much into creating change through the power of networks, so I was delighted when he agreed to let me interview him for this book.

Greg works with organizations to help them drive transformation through change and is one of the most recognized experts on transformational change. His book, *Cascades: How to Create a Movement That Drives Transformational Change* and *Mapping Innovation*, was selected as one of the best business titles of 2017. His work has appeared in such publications as *Harvard Business Review, Barron's, Forbes,* and *Fast Company,* and he was also the co-CEO of the publishing company KP Media. Suffice it to say he knows what he's talking about. I started the interview by asking him what the change process looks like.

"All too often, we look at changes in this sort of linear way. But it doesn't work like that. It starts really, really slow. And then, it accelerates and moves really, really fast. What you often see is a company committing to change. There's a big kickoff meeting, emails going out, they make this event a big thing,

and then a month later, it doesn't seem like really all that much has changed."

I believe this is something we can all relate to. Also, an organization's culture can't change with posters and vision statements on a wall. If the people working at the firm do not relate to the message, the image on the wall is pointless. The culture gets implemented when everyone talks about it and encourages their peers to behave differently.

It would be nice to have a magic formula for change, but it's complex and hard to do. All changemakers must be aware the beginning is the hardest part. Don't announce victory if you have only had your kick-off event. So how does Greg suggest one overcomes that difficult start?

"You have to be able to show the change can be successful. You can't just go to everybody and say, 'Wow, this worked somewhere else; we think this is an excellent idea.' People are naturally hesitant—often because the change hasn't proven itself and because they have other things to do."

It's about showing the change can be successful. This can happen through a small-scale experiment first, and it is about finding enthusiastic individuals who are excited about the proposed change.

You start getting the momentum when you get your small group of early adopters.

THE OBSTACLE: OVERCOMING THE MAJORITY

Greg explained that the people who succeeded in creating a change inside an organization were not the ones who said, "I did this; this is cool," and then other people started to use it. The ones who succeeded were the ones who could excite others, and they would react with, "This is cool; I would like to do that as well."

Let's illustrate this with the digital tech transformation initiative of a multinational consumer goods corporation, Procter and Gamble.

Procter and Gamble created an initiative called *PxG*, which dealt with using digital technologies to solve the organization's research and development (R&D) problems. They started with only one project. According to PxG's head, John Gadsby, "At the beginning, there were just three of us working on a project: one in R&D, one in manufacturing, and one in IT... We knew that we could work together in a better way. Through experimentation and iteration, we reduced the time for a key process from weeks down to hours. That got our work noticed." (Satell, 2020)

We often think that starting small is meaningless, and we all want a significant impact right away. But successful change always begins with a small group loosely connected and united by a shared purpose. As Greg told me, "You have to find their reasons to participate. People adopt change for their reasons, not yours." This is why our mission as a change-maker is to create small groups and bring like-minded people interested in the project in as soon as possible. Those aiming for change should facilitate connections among like-minded people with a sense of shared values and purpose. It is about making everyone proud to be part of the movement; it creates a sense of belonging. If this happens, people will feel empowered and will want to participate.

One of the reasons forming a small group is so essential, Greg told me, is that it helps to overcome the majority. How so? It goes back to a phenomenon identified in the Asch Conformity Experiment (McLeod, 2018).

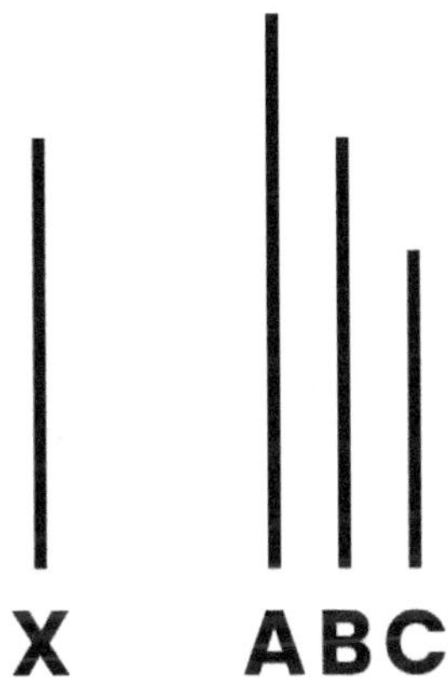

Figure 7.1 Asch Conformity Experiment: Several lines with different heights were presented to the participants.

Solomon Asch, a pioneer of social psychology, conducted a series of experiments during the 1950s. Participants were shown a set of vertical lines labeled X, A, B, and C, and they had to say which line, A, B, or C, was the same length as line X. All participants were Asch's assistants with pre-defined tasks before the experiment, except one. That person didn't know all the other participants were playing along and saying the wrong answer on purpose.

To experiment with how group norms may affect the group members' viewpoint, Asch's assistants said line X was the same length as line A. Even though it was clear that line X was the same length as line B, the participant (the one who was not aware this was an experiment) agreed with the group because the majority said line X was the same length as line A. Asch found that people were willing to ignore reality and provide an incorrect answer to conform to the rest of the group.

We all know it. Usually, we make decisions based on the people surrounding us and often try to fit in. The psychological behavior we learned from this study fundamentally impacts our professional and personal lives. This is why we have to get a few small groups willing to create change to influence and win over the majority.

We know that real change happens when different minds achieve something together. By using effective networks, an incredible impact can be generated. How?

BE AN OPEN BOOK

Have you ever had an idea, but your first intention was to try it out by yourself? Well, I have done this many times.

I am not going to lie to you; I am a failed scientist. What does this mean? I have done over sixteen months of chemical research in academic laboratories in Germany, Switzerland,

and Mexico, but I couldn't publish a scientific paper. I didn't make it. Getting your results published in an academic journal is what motivates most scientists. So, what did I do wrong? Some would say I haven't researched long enough, or that discoveries take time, or that I couldn't do proper research studies. The reality? I didn't collaborate well enough and jumped too many times from one project to another.

I was appointed as the project manager for a research project, and my ego was telling me I could make this discovery by myself. I thought selecting the parameters of my experiment by myself was the brightest idea. Instead, I should have asked more of my colleagues, coworkers, and other scientists from different laboratories what I should do. I did, but not enough.

In Chapter 2 we discussed many studies highlighting that the best ideas come from using a robust, extensive, and diverse network. Two more pieces of research demonstrate how powerful it is:

In the first, Brian Uzzi, Richard L. Thomas Professor of Leadership at the Kellogg School of Management at Northwestern University, was the lead author of the paper, "Atypical Combinations of Scientific Impact," in the journal, *Science*. His team did a quantitative analysis of more than nineteen million scientific papers. They found the most highly cited papers came from specialists in one area collaborating with specialists in entirely different areas. This analysis demonstrates those who worked with peers from different environments were the best scientists who made the most significant discoveries.

Secondly, the 1998 study "Global Theory of Intellectual Change" analyzed the network of philosophers and mathematicians in Asian and Western societies spanning two thousand years. The study showed the secret behind an individual's exceptional creativity was the ability of an individual to tap into their social capital (their network) to gather ideas (Collins, 2000).

Greg said with solid confidence that when you share your idea with your network, you will have a higher probability of coming across a random piece of information or insights that will help you crack a challenging problem! He pointed out, "Breakthrough innovation usually comes across domains." Nevertheless, you can only get those ideas, attract people to your mission, and receive advice from others if you open up. To bring the ideas to you, you have to share the big picture and your challenges. Like scientific discoveries, change can only happen if you talk and ask for feedback.

Charlene Li is an entrepreneur and *New York Times* bestselling author. She has seen business, society, and the world undergo seismic changes. Charlene helps leaders and organizations thrive with disruption and is an expert on digital transformation and leadership. Back when I was in San Francisco in early 2020, I attended the launch of her book, *The Disruption Mindset*. Here's a key quote from the book:

"The major reason people do not buy into a coming change is that they feel uncertain and unsure of what this will mean to them. If they can't understand the change, why it's happening, and how it might affect them, you can't discuss it with them."

According to Charlene, the key to creating change is to be as open and transparent as possible. It builds trust. Charlene, similar to Greg, says being open comes with a shared truth and purpose. Once accomplished, it creates accountability to each other to execute it.

Figure 7.2: Charlene Li and me in San Francisco, 2020 for the launch of her book, The Disruption Mindset, *which mentions the importance of sharing information and being transparent.*

An excellent example to highlight how powerful sharing can be is what Adobe did when it went through a significant digital transformation from 2011 to 2014.

They went from the expensive boxed software with a CD most of you know to a cloud service with a subscription model. Despite the difficulties of transitioning into a completely new business model, they were successful because they focused on transparency with their investment community.

They knew they would lose revenue for a few years until the new cloud service was established. Because of this, many haters were against this long-term strategy and warned them about potential losses. Although they lost a lot in revenue during the start of the transformation, they increased their stock price during the entire shift.

Adobe's CEO can attest that the long-term gains outweigh the short-term challenges. He overcommunicated and was transparent with all its stakeholders: customers, sales representatives, and channel partners (Lev-Ram, 2018). This example is one of many that shows open communication is existential during a crisis and essential transformation.

As Charlene Li puts it:

"What differentiates companies that have successfully adopted disruptive transformation strategies is that they commit to building a relationship through open communication from the start, regardless of the outcome. For Adobe, that meant committing to complete transparency, internally and then externally, from day one." (Li, 2019)

A friend challenged me about this chapter and said he doesn't think being an open book is applicable in the reality of business operations. He believes being an open book will run against you in many cases.

I see where this is coming from. We are so afraid of what other people will do and think about us when we share information that we believe it can cause more damage than opportunities. I disagree; this only applies when someone does the wrong things (corruption, avoiding taxes, overpaying executives, overpaying shareholders and the wrong partners, not delivering on diversity and inclusion, violating human rights, and lobbying). If your business and you are doing the right things, there should be absolutely no fear of sharing openly what you do. Some of my friends and colleagues argued that being open can turn against you. Yes, it can. In general, it's not about being completely open and completely transparent about everything; that is impossible. It's about being open enough so they have enough information to feel connected to us and act, thereby giving them agency. Not sharing anything means we believe the shared information will be used against us, and it also means we don't trust people. Sharing or not sharing sets the type of relationship you want to build with people.

Being an open book helps build networks and people to join a collective goal.

Charlene indicated in her newsletter "How Disruptors Build Trust and Power: that she learned from her research over and over that people want to have honesty and fairness in business. Being an open book helps you to demonstrate you anchor those values. Once you get those two—honesty and fairness—you acquire and build trust.

CONCLUSION

With rapid technological change, the power in today's world is across networks. While it had already been confirmed in the past, it is much more critical today because more people have access to others, and information can be shared more efficiently than ever before.

However, most of us feel we're doing something wrong if we share things with others. Schools told us to do it by ourselves, and we learned that copying someone else is a bad thing. Trying to do it alone will probably lead to nowhere in life and business.

As Greg Satell said, create small groups loosely connected by a shared purpose to make a successful change.

The key to building networks to create and embrace change is to do it collectively because this is how the best ideas can emerge from a combination of atypical minds. Every changemaker will face this situation: Change creates fear. Fear stops our rational brain from operating and rejects all uncomfortable ideas where security and predictability cannot be ensured.

The secret to building networks is to start small, to share information, explain the why, identify the value and purpose of the initiative. It can't work if we don't open up and repeatedly communicate to a selected group of people to overcome the majority and build trust.

TAKE ACTION:

Use all the digital technologies of our time to impact more users faster.

Identify a standard value and purpose to which your idea is connected.

Share: The more you share your ideas and thoughts with your network, the better your impact will be.

To grow and evolve networks, create a small group to facilitate the connections between like-minded people. Organize many events to create the context for people to interact and connect. Use all the tools available such as Yammer, Slack, Teams, newsletters, live meetups, etc.

Make openness and transparency a core principle of your life and implement it in all projects you're involved with. Communicate it with others.

Give access to information—because it builds trust.

Principle 5: Do What You Can't

"Some people see the thing that they want, and some people see the thing that prevents them from getting the thing that they want."

—*SIMON SINEK*

I once watched a video of Simon Sinek, multiple best-selling author and popular public speaker, that truly inspired me. He tells the story of when he and a friend ran in Central Park. At the end of the race, a sponsor gave out free bagels, and a long line of runners waited for their free bagels. Looking at his friend, Simon said, "Let's get a bagel," to which his friend replied, "Nah, the line's too long." Simon responded incredulously, "Free bagel?" "I don't want to wait in line." "Free bagel!" "Nah, too long…"

He realized you can see the world in two ways:

1. You can only see the bagel, i.e., the result—the success, the impact you can create, or
2. You can only see the line—the obstacle.

In the end, he went straight to the box of bagels and got one without waiting in line. Nobody got mad at him because nobody waited longer to get theirs; he did it without disturbing anyone. As Simon said in the video:

"You don't have to wait in line. You don't have to do it the way everyone else has done it. You can do it your way. Break the rules. But you can't get in the way of somebody getting what they want" (Winspire, 2017).

This story illustrates what many of us are facing every day. We often have an idea, and then we see the path to market, the regulations, the competition, and how hard it will be to raise the money to pay people so they can work with us. This is the long line, the obstacles. Most of us get discouraged by it—including me, for some of the projects I started in the past.

However, there is always a way. Sometimes, we can take shortcuts, such as going to other markets or building partnerships to overcome the competition. Some rules can be broken without hurting anyone.

SOME RULES ARE ACTUALLY B******* AND SHOULD BE QUESTIONED

I usually question most of the rules I see. Why? Firstly, often, I don't like them. Second, rules are different everywhere. Usually, they are location-specific and favor only the people living there. If you go to Germany, you will be impressed by how people love rules. Just sit and observe them walk, drive, and commute in cities. Very disciplined. Compared to what I saw when I visited Indonesia in 2016, the world looked completely different. People crossed the streets everywhere. You had five people on one scooter. And everybody was okay with it.

Who's right and who's wrong? Nobody. In my opinion, it's a matter of historical evolution, culture, and politics. Some say we need rules; otherwise, there would be chaos. Yes, we need most of them. However, I invite you to consider that not all rules are equal. We should always ask, *who made the rule, and why?*

- Peter Diamandis, founder and executive chairman of XPRIZE Foundation and founder of Singularity University, named one of the world's fifty most outstanding leaders by Fortune (Peter H. Diamandis LLC, 2022), created a long list of rules to live by, calling them Peter's Laws. Two of them stand out to me: "If you can't win, change the rules," and "If you can't change the rules, ignore them" (SUCCESS, 2016). As Peter puts it, most rules were written in a different era, like when slavery was legal or women couldn't vote. In terms of innovation, many rules are "written to keep the incumbents in charge, blocking innovation" (Diamandis, 2013). Think of the taxi industry blocking Uber from operating.

- Vishen Lakhiani, founder and CEO of Mindvalley and author of *The Code of the Extraordinary Mind*, coined the term *brules*—"bullshit rules." We adopt them to simplify our world understanding, so we don't need to create new ones or nonconform. In doing so, we blindly follow the path everyone has been following for generations to be "normal." We have to set the rules for ourselves and disregard the *brules* preventing us from creating (Lakhiani, 2018).

Without hesitation or doubt, I say the rise of the population connected to the internet will increase global collaboration and make cultures interact more and more. It can make things more complex, and many cultural rules will be challenged. However, it is also an opportunity to remove the rules that do not make sense and make this world more livable, fair, and sustainable for most of us.

When I was studying for my master's degree in chemistry at the University of Freiburg (2016–2019), almost all students from this program did their final internship (master thesis) at the University of Freiburg. Please don't ask me why, but we had to stay at our university. All the students and Ph.D. students told me, "You have to stay here," "You have to pick a research team in Freiburg," etc. However, I was French, and in France, almost all students do their final internships in a company or external research facility. So, I decided to try it because I wanted to experience something I believed was more interesting.

I found a friend who was pursuing her Ph.D. research in Switzerland. She introduced me to the team leader at the Swiss Federal Laboratories for Materials Science and Technology (EMPA), who accepted me as their master's student.

I organized the paperwork, prepared the project, and presented the case to a macromolecular chemistry department professor, who approved it and agreed to be my supervisor. I didn't expect it would be possible, but it was! They were all in favor of making it happen. If I had listened to everybody, I wouldn't have tried, and I would have missed an opportunity that shaped the early days of my career and life.

The secret was to have several stakeholders involved. I could bend the rules with a common purpose, trusted advisors, and a serious topic. Later, many students contacted me and said, "I thought it was impossible; how did you do it?" to which I responded, "Build your relationships." This is one example, but I have done this with many of my projects. I build relationships around a project to make the case stronger to succeed. I involve more people; some of them start to believe it is possible, and then you get the yes.

CHANGEMAKERS HAVE LEARNED WHEN IT'S OKAY TO BREAK THE RULES

Guy Kawasaki, Silicon Valley-based author, speaker, entrepreneur, and tech evangelist, talks about how people will be against you most of the time. As he says in his 2014 TEDx Talk, "Don't Let the Rich, Famous Bozos Drag You Down." He defines the bozos as good people who seem to know everything. However, as he highlights, being successful doesn't mean they are good at predicting the future:

- In 1943, the chairman of IBM, Thomas Watson, said, "I think there is a world market for maybe five computers." A few years later, the world was full of computers.
- A Western Union internal memo from 1876 stated, "This telephone has too many shortcomings to be seriously considered a means of communication. The device is inherently of no value to us." A few decades later, almost everyone had a phone.
- In 1977, Ken Olsen, co-founder of Digital Equipment Corporation, said, "There is no reason why anyone would want a computer in their home." Fast forward a few decades, and almost everyone in the western world has a computer at home.

If you want to change the world, you will swim against the current, and it won't be easy. One of the core qualities any change-maker will need to have is resilience. You will fall on the ground many times. One of the methods to build strength is your ability to think, *with whom can I collaborate* to achieve what everybody tells you can't be done?

CHANGE AGENTS JUST DON'T TAKE NO FOR AN ANSWER—THE STORY OF ALICE AND PATRICIA

Alice Bosley and Patricia Letayf are the co-founders of the startup incubator Five One Labs. They help entrepreneurs in areas affected by conflict to launch their companies by providing training, mentorship, funding, and advisory support. Their vision is to "develop an inclusive network of innovators and entrepreneurs that have the support, skills, and connections to positively change their communities and countries" (Five One Labs, 2022).

Thanks to an introduction by Greg Satell, whom I mentioned in an earlier chapter, I had the opportunity to interview Alice and Patricia. Their story inspired me, as they did something most people wouldn't even dare to think possible. Located in the Kurdistan region of Iraq, they launched in 2017, and by the time I interviewed them in June 2021, their accomplishments include:

- 106 entrepreneurs graduated from their program
- $511,000 in seed funding awarded to Five One Labs, with 56 percent of that going to women entrepreneurs
- Forty-six volunteer mentors and experts in their network globally

Those numbers may look small compared to what entrepreneurs can get in Silicon Valley or Paris, but remember, this is where there was the war. Nothing should logically convince investors to invest there.

In 2017, Kurdistan had an independence referendum. All the airports were shut down by the Iraqi government. Alice was already in Iraq, but Patricia couldn't come in anymore. All borders were shut, and Alice was trapped in Iraq with no money. International money transfers stopped working, and she could only get $1,500 increments from Western Union per day.

When we look at the situation, one wonders why Patricia and Alice would try to do this. Alice was born in the US, and her father was a physician. He moved to Riyadh, Saudi Arabia, in 1997 to work in a hospital with a friend. Alice joined him later with the whole family. Most people would feel this is a bad thing, but as Alice mentioned during the interview:

"I was lucky enough to get to spend time outside of the country throughout my childhood, which is so awesome, especially for Americans. I feel like otherwise, Americans have a hard time understanding the rest of the world."

Alice decided to study international relations with a focus on the Middle East and humanitarian work. Then, she started a job at the American University in the Kurdistan region. There, she was amazed by the abundant motivation and hope of the students. This was "pre-ISIS, pre-drop in oil prices," without that many problems. Later, the situation got worse. Alice felt there was a way to have an impact. She found a way to get her dream job at the UN Refugee Agency in Geneva as an innovation specialist.

"I had the opportunity to create an internal incubator for United Nations colleagues. I proposed that we run an incubator for refugees, and my office said no. So, I decided to quit the UN and go to graduate school [in the US] at Columbia University to study entrepreneurship and innovation in humanitarian settings, specifically in the Middle East. There, I met Patricia."

Patricia comes from a Lebanese family. Her mother and father grew up in Beirut and left during the conflict of the 1970s and 1980s. Before meeting Alice, Patricia had worked as a Middle East political risk analyst and got to know Iraq and the North African region very well. But like Alice, Patricia was frustrated by something:

"After several years, I felt a bit frustrated just because I saw the Islamic State was having a bigger and bigger impact on Iraq and Syria. I became more aware that while I want things to improve in the region, I was also realistic that they were always going to be a challenge. So, I left my job and went to graduate school, where I met Alice."

Alice and Patricia connected because they were both committed to the same mission. Both were frustrated by the number of intelligent and educated people who were ambitious and wanted to have a better life in the Middle East but couldn't do it because of the chaos, the political and socio-economic instability. They decided to be the change. Their mission was to create something unique for the community.

Despite all the obstacles ahead of them, they took the risk. Through building networks, they minimized the problems and increased their resilience.

CHANGEMAKERS LOOK FOR OTHERS TO HELP THEM WITH THE PARTS THEY CAN'T DO

They started this project—building this incubator—when they were at Columbia. They received a little money to do some prototyping (around $5,000). Later, they won the 2017 Columbia Venture Competition SIPA Dean's Challenge and received $15,000 (Startup Columbia, 2021). Shortly after, they received $50,000 from the Tent Foundation, a non-profit

organization made of a coalition of businesses that have committed to take action to help refugees. In addition to this, they
also received several smaller amounts of funding. In total,
they had raised over $90,000 for their first year. However,
even with that funding, they were underfunded. But they
wanted to launch anyway.

At the beginning, they were exhausted. Patricia and Alice
were trying to raise funds for their initiative independently.
In addition to the political turmoil, it was the very first incubator program in Iraq, and no one knew what an incubator
was. "It just felt like there was no way this would ever become
anything," Alice mentioned. "My dad was calling me on the
phone: 'You're starving to death; you're not paying yourself.
What are you doing?'"

It's at this point that most people stop. They quit, give up.
But not Alice and Patricia. They kept going because "there
was no other option." "But how did you make it through?"
I asked. She said they realized they needed more money
to survive and started putting all their efforts into building partnerships.

- They received free co-working space through one
  partnership.
- They ended up getting free internet through another
  association.
- They received funding from the US Embassy in Bagdad.
  They achieved this by inviting the US consul to many
  of their events. The consul supported them and encouraged them to apply for funding that the US Embassy was
  offering

- They partnered with the International Organization for Migration, an agency of the United Nations agency.

Alice and Patricia admitted, "We leaned on partnerships, building out these collaborations that ended up paying off in the long run. Our success attracted other donors, and eventually, the political situation calmed down."

It worked out because all those stakeholders were inspired by their mission and intention. It was a network effect; many more wanted to help so Alice and Patricia could accomplish their goal.

CONCLUSION

In this chapter, we learned there will always be rules and obstacles in our way; there is almost no chance of avoiding them. Rules, most of the time, were set in a different time for specific purposes. Many are questionable. As Simon Sinek said, "Some people see the things that they want; some people see the things that prevent them from getting what they want" (Winspire, 2017).

Any person in the world will face resistance when introducing a new idea, and successful business people understand *when* it is the time to bend a rule. More broadly, successful people just don't take no for an answer. They find a way; they focus on the goal, not the obstacles.

Wishful thinking does not lead anywhere. The last part is to form powerful alliances, by identifying those who share the same problems, values, and identity. And by building networks and forming partnerships with individuals and organizations. Patricia and Alice did that and succeeded in overcoming the countless challenges. In early 2021 Alice and Patricia were named "Columbia University Entrepreneurs of the Year," which highlights and validates their brilliant accomplishments so far.

Many parts of the world still live in extreme conditions and political instability. However, there is hope: Today's world evolves as a connected network. There has never been a better time to build something *anywhere*—by receiving support from *anywhere*. This can be done by simply running a crowd-funding campaign on Indiegogo or Kickstarter or applying for grants. In Germany, all regional states provide capital to start a business; equity capital is also available with KFW (German state-owned investment and development bank), which offers loans. In France, BPI does the same ("Banque Publique d'Investissement," also called the one-stop-shop for entrepreneurs). Worldwide, you can apply to count-less startup competitions to get funded, such as EIT (the European Institute of Innovation and Technology), EXIST (a funding program provided by the Federal Ministry for Economic Affairs and Energy, in Germany), or in the US, the XPRIZE Foundation.

Building networks is the power of our time. By doing what you can't, anyone can establish partnerships and overcome the odds. You can resist and thrive during the most chal-lenging time if you're able to build relations. Political crises or pandemics, networks help you to get through anything.

<u>*TAKE ACTION:*</u>

To start with some great inspiration, watch Casey Nei-stat's YouTube video, "DO WHAT YOU CAN'T."

If you have a project and there are rules or regulations standing in your way, ask yourself, Who made them? How can I overcome them?

Find out who is having the same issues. Who believes it should be changed? Connect with them.

Identify your mission and find a way to inspire others. This is the most important reason people will work with you. What's your WHY?

Find and choose your promising partners. Ask for intro-ductions and highlight the reasons why they should care about it.

Once you find your partner, build relationships for the long term. Make them feel they were an extraor-dinary part of the journey. Otherwise, they will only help you once.

CHAPTER 9

Principle 6: Go Viral

---

*"This is the beauty of social media: it
helps you find people and then you can
contact them fast and inexpensively."*

—GUY KAWASAKI

I couldn't write this book without talking about this essential tool for building networks, innovating, and influencing society by creating a movement: social media. I love social media. I've often been criticized for using it too much, being called "the LinkedIn guy" ("He just writes posts all day"). Yet I know many professionals who avoid it because they think it is not part of their job, or because it's presumed to be a waste of time. They assume social media is only for non-business-related activities, or they think it's only for consultants, salespeople, and marketing gurus.

Most of you probably know Guy Kawasaki. After graduating from Stanford University, he worked closely with Steve Jobs in the early days of Apple Macintosh. Since then, he's worked at Google, Mercedes Benz, and today he is the chief evangelist officer of Canva, the app we all use to make excellent images. It's fair to say he's a prominent—and respected—voice in the technology space. When writing this book, he had over four hundred thousand fans on Facebook, 1.4 million followers on Twitter, and three million followers on LinkedIn. And as co-author of the book, *The Art of Social Media*, it's fair to say he is someone worth listening to when it comes to social media. He uses it to connect with countless people worldwide to build successful companies, attract talent, and collaborate. And he's not alone.

The truth is, in today's digital world, with the increase in remote work, social media enables collaboration for anyone working in teams and with partners.

SOCIAL MEDIA IN THE WORLD TODAY

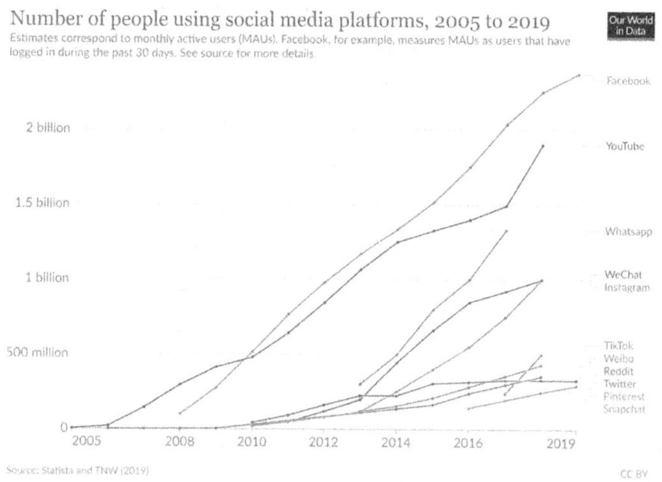

Today, of a global population of 7.7 billion people, a minimum of 3.5 billion people are online. According to Esteban Ortiz-Ospina, a senior researcher and head of operations at *Our World in Data*, "Social media has changed the world. The rapid and vast adoption of these technologies is changing how we find partners, how we access information from the news, and how we organize to demand political change."

Two-thirds of all internet users use social media, and as we can see in Figure 9.1, nearly a third of the world connects to at least one platform: Facebook. I get 90 percent of my news through social media and connect daily with new people. Every day I see viral posts going around that call out for a change.

In June 2021, Mike Holston, an Instagrammer with more than six million followers, posted a tragic photo of the last white rhino on the planet, dead on the ground. The caption read, "The northern white rhino which survived fifty-five million years...was a testament to numerous historical changes on the planet [but] could not survive humans. The post got over ten million views, with over one million likes. In the post's description, Michael linked to the BioRescue Project, a non-profit organization whose mission is to save the Northern White Rhinos from extinction.

Vishen Lakhiani, founder and CEO of Mindvalley, also uses his vast social media presence to create change in the world. A video denouncing the sugar content of Coca-Cola received over thirty million views (Lakhiani, 2020). Another video about the amount of sugar in Nestlé's products for kids in Malaysia received over 1.2 million views in 2018 and more than eight million views in 2020 (Lakhiani, 2020). It pushed Nestlé to issue press releases explaining the content of its products to the public.

Both Holston and Lakhiani use social media to make our world a better place to live in. But here's the thing: You don't need to be an influencer to use it effectively. *Anyone can.*

I've been an early adopter of most social media platforms. I've tried them all: Facebook, Snapchat, Instagram, Flickr, LinkedIn, Twitter, YouTube, TikTok, and more recently, Clubhouse. In the beginning, I used Facebook, Snapchat, and Instagram only for travel content when, in 2015, I shared my journey through Africa on Facebook. Here, people could discover this beautiful content with me as I traveled through eight countries over five months. I shared weekly videos and posted pictures daily. It felt like I had a community; many people wanted to know more. So, when I returned, I gave presentations about my travels at schools and to other audiences.

But social media for professional content, is it possible? Of course, it is.

SOCIAL MEDIA FOR SCIENCE, INNOVATION, AND BUSINESS

In 2017, I participated in a national chemical communication contest called The Chemical World Tour in France. We worked with one of the biggest press agencies in the country,

CAPA and France Chimie. Our goal was to spread the beauty of science to a broad audience, and one of the videos we recorded was at Bayer in Lyon, France, showing the laboratory of the future (ChemicalWorldTour, 2017). We made extensive use of social media, reaching over hundreds of thousands of views throughout the contest.

My team won the contest with eight thousand votes that we gathered in just three weeks with the help of the Internet and our networks. A prominent French magazine, *20 Minutes*, covered the initiative on its second page with the headline, "When a Student Is on a Mission to Popularize Chemistry" (Ighirri, 2017). The magazine was distributed to tens of thousands of people. The entire world helped us win the contest and share the beauty of chemistry. That was the moment I understood the impact social media can have. It can create a movement.

However, social media is not only for winning contests. It can help accelerate the revenue of a company as well. At the moment, the best platform in Europe and the US by far is LinkedIn.

Jason Miller, a UK-based brand marketer whose resume includes positions held at Microsoft and LinkedIn mentions:

"Sharing content raises your employees' profiles, pushing them to the front of people's minds when it comes to new opportunities, and establishing their expertise. There's real value in this for any professional."

Research from LinkedIn shows that when employees share content, they typically see a click-through rate double that of their company. Even though only 3 percent of employees share content, they generate 30 percent of all content engagement for a typical business (Miller, 2017). By posting, everybody wins.

TODAY'S WORKFORCE IS ONLINE; LINKEDIN IS A WAY TO CONNECT DEEPER WITH YOUR TEAM, COLLABORATORS, AND CLIENTS

I am not the only non-marketing person who recognizes the importance of social media when collaboration is required.

Granny&Smith is a boutique innovation agency specializing in innovation acceleration. I came across Lars Behrendt, the CEO (though he prefers to be called an innovation engineer), on LinkedIn. His posts caught my attention as his slide decks contained over a hundred and fifty pages! I'd rarely seen something similar before. I started following him and liked and commented on his posts. During one of his webinars, I asked some questions he didn't answer live, so he sent me a private message afterward to apologize and suggested we meet for a virtual coffee chat. Because I was working on similar projects, we wanted to see how we could collaborate and help each other. Since our initial call, Lars and I have stayed in touch, and we've had several calls despite our busy lives. We both agree; it feels like we know each other, even though we've never met in person!

In 2020, during the COVID-19 pandemic, his European clients froze his projects; many were canceled. He decided to go international, "working the network." Using social media extensively, they secured big clients and built a global team. He went from around five thousand followers across platforms to fifty thousand followers in just one year. When writing this book, he had over sixty thousand followers on LinkedIn alone. Naturally, I wanted to interview Lars for this book to get an insight into why he is so active on social media and why he thinks others should care about it in today's digitally networked world.

Lars and his team have worked with hundreds of clients during the past fifteen years. He has worked with Fortune 500 and DAX companies such as BMW, Linde, Volkswagen, T-Mobile, IBM, Siemens, Konica Minolta, and Allianz. As you can imagine, Granny&Smith need to find new clients all the time. I was curious to hear what has changed in how he has worked during the past few years.

The first time Lars used video calls was in the year 2000. At that time, it felt like a revolution, but almost all his meetings were still happening in the office. He believed people had to be physically present to run workshops. On top of this, Lars also highlighted how complicated it was to get new clients back then. He needed to drive to companies, wear a black suit, present professional slides with strong branding about the agency. "It was so different; it took months to get new clients. Today, it's not B2B or B2C anymore; it's human to human again. It's changed so drastically; now, it's through digital networking."

Lars insists that we seek intensive connection with people again, not with brands. "That's what has changed; we don't trust brands anymore, not as much as we used to. The best brand is your personality."

Ninety-nine percent of all the types of projects and workshops that were conducted in person back in 2000 have switched through virtual engagements. He was wholly convinced that in-person interactions are essential, but the COVID-19 lockdowns proved the opposite. He was astonished; he never thought it would work so well. He realized that from placing a project, working as a team, and bringing it to the market can be done 100 percent online.

Today, the innovation agency has a designer in Kyiv, a software developer in Bangladesh, and a few core members in Germany. Now, when new German clients call Lars and ask him to come over to Munich, Lars tells them he doesn't want to lose a day to travel back and forth; he kindly suggests a virtual chat of thirty minutes instead. The situation has changed so much that companies are comfortable with this new format, saving Lars considerable time.

We are currently experiencing a massive shift in how we work, interact, and do business. More global teams, more international projects, lower travel costs, better access to talent, and faster implementation of ideas. The so-called go-to-market is also quicker, as interacting online can connect you with the right partners. Social media is an indispensable tool in today's multistakeholder economy!

BUILDING NETWORKS USING SOCIAL MEDIA BY OVER-COMING FEAR

Engaging on social media is like networking live but with an effect times 1,000. Instead of talking to one person with your message, you speak to thousands. Lars expressed how impressed he was by this new tool: "Digital networking is a new superpower because it is new; I mean it. I believe we are still at the beginning."

The secret? Using the tool.

Lars and I both believe countless intelligent people underuse it. Many still believe you only use it if you need to sell something or need a job. Unfortunately, marketing and salespeople are the ones who use it the most. As Lars pointed out, "Where are all those engineers?"

I wondered why this resource remains untapped by so many people around us. People are reluctant to use it because they fear rejection and failure (i.e., fear that no one will like the post). On top of it, the excuse I hear the most is that it is a waste of time. Yes, it takes some time, but it comes back when you see how much we receive in return from the effort. The biggest obstacle for most people when it comes to posting is overthinking. Some say it is for privacy reasons, but even that is often an excuse for not posting.

Moreover, I know most people target perfection, which is useless on social media. I can tell you, between a meme with a great joke and message, a selfie video made in two minutes, and a perfect expensive video, the meme and the quickly made video will probably win on social media and receive more views. It's about sharing something relatable and adds value to people's lives. Money doesn't create quality on those platforms. The audience will tell you what quality is with their engagement, and it is often not what you think.

Lars recommended to a friend that he should post a video on LinkedIn to improve his branding. Lars taught his friend what to say and how to record. Once it was time to post the video, his friend objected: "No, I can't do it; I need a better camera, a better lighting; it's not perfect." Lars was impressed with all these excuses. "He was completely freaking out. People have to show the outside world what they stand for; show their personality. If they do not stand for anything, that's fine, but then don't expect something magical to happen."

Lars and I post every day on LinkedIn, and we both know it doesn't make sense to overthink. During our conversation, we both agreed that when you look at the profile of someone who liked one of your posts and says what they care about, you feel you can trust them because you know a bit about who they are.

SOCIAL MEDIA TO BUILD TRUST AND BONDING

My boss once told me, "I can screen a candidate's resume and advise you in twenty seconds if it is a good fit." Our attention span has decreased due to the use of social media. In today's scroll culture we have twenty seconds to present ourselves and give our first impression—offline and online.

Posting is a way to show who we are, what we do, and what we believe in repeatedly to thousands of users. The people who post get an unfair advantage because more people will trust them faster.

As Lars mentioned, "For me, it starts getting strange when people do not post anything or do not like anything. I do not know who they are. I can't understand what they want if I do not see anything from them. If you are serious about doing business, you must show some of your personality to the outside world. This is what is changing today compared to before. I strongly believe that soon you will not stand a chance without using social media. Just have an outstanding idea and share it."

Social media is not about likes, follower count, and ego. It is about connecting with people and establishing trust. Lars recently had a call with a person in the US whom he had never met nor interacted with before. When the call started, the guy said, "You don't have to explain anything. I know you very well. I read in all your posts, and I have a pretty good understanding of what kind of guy you are."

This is the power of social media. It helps you to be an open book, which is one of the secrets to bonding with people in today's digital and networked world. Curious to know if this was only my experience or if other people could relate, I asked the question in some of my closed communities: "Why do you use social media?" Here are some of the responses:

- Being online is the best way to attract new community members/followers to spread the word about whatever you're passionate about. After a lot of resistance, I accept that social presence is necessary to move a movement forward in this day and age.

- Being online creates a sense of connection to my people.
- It attracts partners, clients, and talents.
- Often in my work, I reach out to potential clients, and if other partners see my content and share my values, once we get on a Zoom call, there is massive trust and bonding to speed up business and expansion.
- And my favorite one: Once we get on a Zoom call, there is massive trust and bonding.

Being active on social media is not just for fun; it is a must. Nobody will force you to use it, but it's like a giant microphone you are either using or not. This microphone can be used to get feedback on an idea you have. It can also be used to ask for help, educate your audience about a topic, and attract talent to apply.

CONCLUSION

If you want to create change globally, having an idea is not sufficient. You need to be able to scale to make an impact. Social media is an extremely powerful tool for sharing a message and attracting talent to your mission. I have seen many instances of people going viral on LinkedIn, getting ten thousand likes with only a thousand followers. It is your opportunity to share a message you care about with the world.

I connect with people through social media every day, either for a project or to catch up, and I hear the same message: "Keep posting videos of the events you are going to; they are amazing" or "Thanks for the posts; they're so inspiring."

What is the lesson here? There is little to lose by being active on social media and gaining so much.

So, why are so many still so skeptical about it?

First, there is the erroneous belief that social media only shares cat videos with random content and accelerates the spread of misinformation. Secondly, many say it's a waste of time and a distraction from the actual work. Thirdly, some only start being active when looking out for a job. And lastly, many are angry about receiving messages from salespeople (especially on LinkedIn) and believe that's the only thing it's used for.

The secret to benefiting from social media is to post regularly instead of being a consumer. Your entire perspective will change. You will begin to receive insightful comments and messages from people interested in knowing more about the work you do. You will increase the rate of sales for your company and attract the right people to your mission. Last but not least, if you're able to meet in person after interacting with people online for a long time, the human bond is compelling. I experienced this many times, and many of my friends shared the same feeling.

By reading this chapter, I hope you understood that being on social media is not for travel anymore. It is an essential tool to innovate and create change through networks. It builds an ecosystem around you, your company, and your mission.

Discover your social selling index score on LinkedIn at https://www.linkedin.com/sales/ssi. As of February 2022, I am in the top 1 percent in the industrial SSI rank and top 2 percent in the network SSI rank. How about you?

The best way to be inspired is to analyze what other influencers, like Gary Vaynerchuk, Brené Brown, Mark Cuban, and Arianna Huffington, are doing. Replicate what they do for your journey.

Take a class and learn from the best. For example, the LinkedIn course by Guy Kawasaki, "How to Rock Social Media," or "altMBA" by Seth Godin.

If you're unwilling to do the work yourself, hire a free-lancer on fiverr to give you a marketing plan to start (it can cost as little as twenty dollars).

Stop the fear by taking action.

CHAPTER 10

Principle 7: Be Bold and Have Skin in the Game!

"To be successful in business and investing, you've got to have skin in the game, a stake in the company."

—WARREN BUFFETT

When Steve Jobs, co-founder of Apple, and his team launched the legendary marketing campaign "Think Different" in 1997, they wanted to remind everyone of their brand's core value: passionate people willing to change the world. It also showed they deeply cared about their employees who dared to be different. "The crazy ones" were the company's heroes. The text of the campaign says it all:

"Here's to the crazy ones. The misfits. The rebels. The trouble-makers. The round pegs in the square holes. The ones who see things differently. They're not fond of rules and they have no

respect for the status quo. You can quote them, disagree with them, glorify or vilify them. About the only thing you can't do is ignore them. Because they change things. They push the human race forward. And while some may see them as the crazy ones, we see genius. Because the people who are crazy enough to think they can change the world are the ones who do" (Harry Piotr, 2013).

Was Steve Jobs and Apple right? Do we need more rebels and bold thinkers to change the world? Yes. As Jeff Dyer and Hal Gregersen point out in their *Harvard Business Review* article, "Learn How to Think Different(ly)," great innovators (launching new businesses, products, and processes) excel at connecting the unconnected using associational thinking. They spend almost 50 percent more time thinking differently than non-innovators.

Is this art of thinking a talent, or can you train yourself to think differently?

A study of over 5,000 entrepreneurs and executives found that almost anyone who consistently makes an effort to think differently can think differently (Dyer and Gregersen, 2011). You can train yourself to live with this philosophy.

If it is evident that being different and bold helps a company, yourself, and the world, why wouldn't more people do it? As Harvard Medical School's researchers found, 60 to 80 percent experienced being uncomfortable and even exhausted when thinking differently (Carson, 2010). But while being different and thinking differently from the rest is hard, this chapter should remind you about the incredible benefits you do.

DARE TO BE DIFFERENT

Until I was fifteen years old, I wasn't interested in being a good student, and I wouldn't say I liked school. My grades were around seven to ten out of twenty (equivalent to D or B grades in the US), and I was one of the lowest-performing students in my class. My parents didn't study themselves and couldn't help me much with my homework. Sometimes they were upset when I got terrible grades. Sometimes they forgot about it. The remarks in my school report said it all:

- "He must learn to organize his work. I am waiting for more dedication. Make an effort."
- "The work is too irregular. Mikel is not concentrating enough, and there is no perseverance to learn from the lessons."
- "Weak results, little participation."

When I reflect on this time, I remember I was not affected emotionally. I didn't care; I was living my life as if everything had been going well for years. I was okay with being a misfit, which may be why I still think differently today, and I am not afraid of it. At work or in my personal life, I try new things every day, like posting on social media, asking questions at town hall meetings, proposing topics for the next team meeting, or reaching out without fear to top executives or famous people. I do things, and people often express they're impressed by my mindset. Sometimes it gets me into trouble. While they may feel insecure about my behavior at first, they eventually trust me.

My former manager, Chris Haskell, formerly vice president at Bayer Pharmaceuticals, told me in a one-to-one meeting at our offices in San Francisco that initially, he was unsure about my work capabilities. He said I was "all over the place," trying to implement so many ideas in different projects that he didn't know if he could let me pursue the projects by myself or if he needed to monitor and support me all the time. He wasn't sure if I was focused enough on my tasks. However, at the end of my assignment, he gave me this recommendation:

"Mikel is VERY passionate about innovation, brought so much energy and great ideas to our group [...] Bayer needs more people like him—willing to challenge the status quo and just ask, 'Why not?' Mikel is a professional networker that uses the power of communication and collaboration to accelerate outcomes. I do not doubt that Mikel will be a future global empathetic and disruptive leader that can share a vision and motivate his team around him."

The same thing happened with my current employer. When I joined the team consisting of five Japanese people, I gave all my ideas and challenged the status quo. When my probation period was almost finished, I received feedback they considered firing me because I wasn't leaning to the group's thinking and sometimes it was disturbing the harmony of the team. The biggest problem is that it was a monoculture. Later on, after a new boss had joined and the team became more diverse with people from India and Germany, the situation improved as the team became more culturally diversified. My different way of thinking was finally more accepted, and more people started to also express their opinions in meetings. The whole team started to challenge each other's ideas, with respect and acceptance. It was the perfect sign that we were establishing a culture of an innovative team.

My new boss recently said, "Most people would give up their ideas when facing rejection, but you just don't care. One of the things you have is an exceptional mindset."

If I have this mindset today, it is because I met countless individuals who convinced me it was okay to think differently. One of the people I followed and met in person is Naveen Jain.

BE THIRSTY, BOLD, CURIOUS, AND ASK QUESTIONS

Naveen Jain is the perfect example of being bold and successful. Naveen is the founder of seven companies, whose success led to him being a billionaire. He is a "moonshot thinker," the dreamer, the disruptor. He talks to the younger generation through numerous channels, including podcasts, TEDx Talks, and online courses. He teaches his audience about the importance of being bold and how to solve the world's biggest problems. I first learned about Naveen from Dave Asprey's book, *Game Changers: What Leaders, Innovators, and Mavericks Do to Win at Life.* I listened to several interviews and watched videos about him on YouTube, and I took his Mindvalley class, "The Power of Boldness." I fell in love with his passion, energy, and mindset.

Figure 10.3: Me with Naveen Jain at a conference in Silicon Valley in 2019, talking about how to find your moonshot and the importance of being bold.

I'm sure we all know the saying, "You can lead a horse to water, but you can't make it drink." When someone doesn't want to do something, you cannot do much for them. What I learned from Naveen is the focus should be on making the horse thirsty. The thirst and curiosity that Naveen evokes enable him to build massive companies impacting billions of lives. His relentless curiosity is what made Naveen succeed in several disciplines. Because he is not an expert, he allowed himself to be bold, and ask "crazy," challenging questions of the people working with him in the different projects he was working on.

A 2019 article by Rafael Badziag tells of when Naveen and his team met with Bill Gates. "I was in my first few months at Microsoft, and we were in a meeting about Windows NT; I was just a mid-level manager—the dumb young guy." In the middle of the presentation, Gates turned to Naveen and asked him what he thought of the operating system. "Bill, I think it's going to be big, fat, and slow." Everybody stayed silent. Naveen continues, "All the top guys were in that meeting. And Bill Gates was an extremely intense person. He quietly looked at me for ten seconds and then said, 'Exactly!'"

Afterward, Naveen's manager took him aside and said, "Do you know you work for me? And what you did is absolutely going to cost you." Naveen replied, "Martin, it may come as a surprise to you, but I do not work for you. I work for the company, and I work for myself. So don't you ever tell me I work for you." Naveen's manager put him on probation, saying, "That will show you whom you work for."

As it turns out, this act of boldness helped the company. "They changed everything in that operating system to become a lean, mean operating system. All because I was able to say, 'Bill, this is exactly what's going to happen if you go down this path.'"

The most important lesson Naveen points out from such experience is this one:

"So the cost was that I almost got fired. But that's how entre-preneurs are. They don't care. They're going to say what they believe, and then they're going to go out and do it themselves" *(Badziag, 2019).*

Change-makers have to be accustomed to being uncomfortable when presenting a new idea or a new process. Most people will reject it at first. This is also why thinking differently is a painful and awkward situation. The key is to communicate as much as possible about why we believe the new idea is excellent and show its long-term impact. Once you establish trust with your manager and the people around you, you can finally "be yourself."

Creating change happens by starting with an act of boldness. Be willing to take risks, act innovatively, have confidence, have courage, and be okay with being different. You stop wondering if you are upsetting someone in the room in this state of mind. However, saying things out loud is not enough. Being bold can be turned against you unless you can execute your ideas. It is essential to measure the progress along the way and demonstrate early results. In the end, you want more people to join you to grow and accelerate the impact. Let's learn from another Indian-born change-maker who shared a similar story to Naveen.

HAVE SKIN IN THE GAME—THE STORY OF JAYKANT.

I had the pleasure of interviewing Jaykant Patel, founder of ARCHETYPE Investments, a US-based real estate company. ARCHETYPE went from zero to over a hundred million dollars in asset value in just six years, with another couple hundred million in the pipeline. As founder and managing principal, Jaykant—Jay—leads the sourcing, negotiation, and execution of the firm's growing portfolio.

Jay represents the typical American dream. He immigrated with his parents from India when he was just one year old. Even though his parents were educated—his father has a master's degree and his mom was a teacher—they had to start at the bottom of the ladder again in the US. His father had to be a janitor in hospitality, and his mom was a housekeeper in a motel.

Jay told me, "I received the work ethic from my parents. They also took a lot of risks. In life, you have to take risks, and they did. So, you know, it is partially my genetic code. That's what drives you when you're raised in such a manner." He and his family have grown from humble beginnings into respectable success. His parents sent him to law school, among the most prestigious educations possible in the US.

I found the story insightful because it is true that your parents have a tremendous influence on you. In his book *Outliers*, Malcolm Gladwell highlights the success stories of immigrants, where the children ended up very successful because of the parents' work ethic. Similarly, my mom also started as a housekeeper. She had grown up in a low-income family forced to immigrate from Poland to Germany during World War II. Her family lost everything because the Germans stole all her family's farms and land in the country. Today, even in her late fifties, she is the most motivated and positive person I know. Her energy was transferred to me as well.

I wanted to understand how Jay built such extensive networks to access better ideas, resources such as real estate deals, and the best people and partners to fulfill his vision. The impact he and his team has made on the real estate market around North Carolina and South Carolina in just a few years is substantial, and we can learn many lessons from this for many other industries.

We started our discussion, and right away, we discussed how relationships are essential to scale a business. Jay mentioned that early on from his investment and banking experience, he learned that managing relationships and networking were critical in getting deals done. "The people that win the deal are the ones that can navigate through different networks and relationships."

Today, when Jay and his team see an opportunity to invest and get a deal, the first question they ask is, "What relationships exist in our team that we can leverage to make sure that we get to the right players that are going to be involved in this deal?" His firm has a long list of contacts they continuously update. When they need it, they screen it and detect which person could help them get the desired deal done.

You may wonder, *How does Jay keep his network warm?* When he schedules his days and months, he always tries to put some time aside to reach out to one investor or banker each day, five to seven days per week. The call is usually not about selling or asking but simply making sure they're okay. He will call them if he hasn't talked to them in a while. Sometimes, it is about sending an email. He does that to remind them they can reach him anytime and access him directly, even as the company grows. "I think it helps a lot. I think that keeps the relationship growing and nurtured."

Jay admitted that not everything went smoothly in all his projects. He cited an example of the purchase of his second asset when he let a third party evaluate maintenance work or deferred maintenance to reconstruct the buildings. These costs were not calculated correctly, and he and his team had to put in millions to stabilize the asset after they realized much more maintenance work had to be done on the building. He admitted, "I didn't leverage my very close network and the contacts that I trust to give me opinions." Later, everything was fine, and they could sell it for twice the amount they had invested. Jay acknowledged he wasn't *resourceful* in this situation. Today, he always asks several people in his network before making financial decisions.

He doesn't only build networks for his business; he reaches out to his relationships because he knows they are also a source of information. He uses them as a resource. "We have investors who are doctors, lawyers, some other developers, and whatnot. So, I like to learn about what they see in their industry and their markets. Same with bankers; I want to see what deals they're seeing and how they're pricing them, etc."

Another thing that differentiates Jay from other real estate developers and his competition is that he always wants to be the majority investor in all his projects or, as he says, have the most skin in the game. "Unlike other developers, who throw in 5 percent or 10 percent equity and charge a lot of fees to the project for their services, I like to be the majority investor in every project."

CREDIBILITY + RELIABILITY = ACCOUNTABILITY

By taking the most risks and showing the results, ARCHE-TYPE Investments built trust with the banks and stakeholders. I asked Jay why this is important. "By being the majority investor, I'm going to be very meticulous about our decisions, how we structure the project, and how we build the project." He added, "It also makes everyone in the project sleep easy at night."

The key to growing Jay's network was using a different philosophy than many other people have in this business. While most like to tell their investors everything will be great when the project starts and then stay silent when it goes wrong, Jay insists he will do everything he can not to lose his investor's money when it goes wrong. "Knock on wood; that's my key thing," he said with confidence. Thanks to this philosophy, investors are keen to work with him.

In other words, to build a network of knowledge, resources such as financial data, and people to work with you, you must be accountable.

Like Jay, you need to show your stakeholders you will do everything you can to make the project succeed. Jay highlighted, "I've never made a capital call after initial investments, which I pride myself on. And I never want to make a capital call." Jay stated, with conviction, if they run out of budget and additional capital is needed, he will take the responsibility to add what is necessary. According to him, this helped them grow their investor base organically.

You have to do what you said you would do! What is the magic formula of accountability? Credibility + Reliability = Accountability.

These three factors are all interdependent. If one goes down, it affects the other. How can you be sure these three factors are always as high as possible?

The bigger the project's significance, the more extensive network of people you will need to make your vision a reality and capable of scaling. And as we learned from Jay, the investors and stakeholders critical to your mission need to be able to come to you without too much effort. This only happens when you create a brand of yourself—by having skin in the game and succeeding in your first projects.

CONCLUSION

Today, we live in a noisy world, and many get overwhelmed by the information they get. Telling people *what* you do is not enough. The *why* is much more relevant. Steve Jobs and Apple launched the Think Different campaign in 1997 because they wanted to communicate their top values.

The message here is that the most incredible change-makers in our world started with a bold idea. Every single one of them was challenged by others and faced painful rejections. To overcome and go from an idea to implementation, and scaling is to explain the *why*, and show you are willing to do whatever it takes: being bold, taking risks, and have skin in the game. It's also not just about your numbers in the business; it is a mindset. These people do not blame others for failures; they take responsibility.

When you live this philosophy, you build credibility, reliability, and therefore, accountability.

The rest is all about the network effect. You'll attract the best people—the ones who are qualified and capable of accomplishing complicated tasks. You'll also get access to the best information and the best deals. Challenging times will be avoided, your return on investments will be higher, your time will be saved, and the impact will be much more significant.

By being bold and by having skin in the game, you grow the following networks:

- Network of knowledge and ideas to be inspired, test hypotheses, and improve your project, product, goal.
- Network of resources such as capital (revenue, debt, equity, grant financing), infrastructure, legal, marketing, administrative, databases, etc.
- Network of people to join you, work with you and help you accomplish your goals and mission.

We need more changemakers willing to take the risks to change—in many cases outdated systems—and create a positive change in the world.

Be curious and re-question everything. Don't be afraid to challenge the status quo.

Trust yourself, and express thought leadership. Asking questions and saying what you truly believe in team meetings has more advantages than disadvantages.

Update your contact list continuously. Start building one today, and set monthly reminders to reach the top people of your networks to refresh the connections. Social media is also a great way to keep the network warm (see Chapter 9).

Have skin in the game, and show you're willing to take the most risks in a project. It will build your reliability and credibility and, as a result, develop your accountability.

PART 3

WHAT IS NEXT

CHAPTER 11

Future Outlook

———

"Profit for a company is like oxygen for a person. If you don't have enough of it, you're out of the game. But if you think your life is about breathing, you're really missing something."

—PETER F. DRUCKER

We can all think of a time when we gave up. Maybe it was at school, an exam. Perhaps at work, after fighting and struggling to keep a project going. Or it could be in a sport when the competitors were more robust and better, or it might be when you supported a political cause. While defeat always feels terrible, you might agree that giving up is easy. It's much harder to feel overwhelmed and persevere until the challenge is over and the problem is solved. You are reading this now, at the end of the book, which tells me you are genuinely committed to creating a difference in people's lives and ready to impact the world.

This book is published at a time of extreme tensions world-wide. Everything is continuing to speed up while existential challenges are growing. The pandemic that started in 2020 has shined a light on many critical problems of our society. We saw governments unable to work together, with confusing messages and regulations across countries, decreasing the trust of its citizens. We saw a financial system that benefits the wealthiest as trillions of dollars landed in the most prosperous hands while an additional 120 million people fell under the extreme poverty line (Ferreira, 2021). The 2020 report, "Fires, Forests, and the Future: A Crisis Raging Out of Control?" by the World Wildlife Fund and Boston Consulting Group, shows that our planet is nearing its limit. Humans cause 75 percent of wildfires, and the number of fire alerts around the world in 2020 was up 13 percent compared to 2019—which was already a record year. If we don't act now, our world will become even less sustainable, more unequal, and more fragile. A few days before this book was sent to my publisher for copy editing, a war started in Ukraine, which some called the potential beginning of World War III (Boyd, 2022). One of the world's pressing issues is social cohesion, so I hope this book with help and provide people these mindset principles so more collaborations can be formed. It is only cooperatively that we will overcome these grand challenges.

However, there is a lot of hope. Albert Einstein once said, "In the midst of every crisis lies great opportunity" (Goodreads, 2022). And here is ours. Today is our chance to change the system; it is our opportunity to build a better world together. Everybody knows decisions taken with a purely top-down approach from isolated actors, public or private, are not enough. Change has to come from all citizens of the planet:

activists, scientists, artists, athletes, teachers, engineers, lawyers, doctors and nurses, construction workers, politicians, and anyone else working hard every day.

THE CRISIS IS AN OPPORTUNITY TO CHANGE AND RESET CAPITALISM

The World Economic Forum called its fiftieth annual conference "The Great Reset." Public and private leaders came together in 2020 to discuss how to rebuild our society and economy.

Three focuses were identified (Schwab, 2020):

1. Creating the condition for a "stakeholder economy," which is about new policies, tax reforms, trade arrangements, and more to boost public-private partnerships and increase collaboration across businesses.
2. Investments to advance shared goals, such as equality and sustainability.
3. Harnessing the innovations of the fourth industrial revolution, social and health challenges being the priorities.

They highlighted the need to reduce our *shareholder capitalism*, which reinforces the priority of making profits for shareholders alone, and that instead, we will move toward *stakeholder capitalism*. The focus is on gains in this economy and works with a new dashboard encompassing people, the planet, prosperity, and institutions (World Economic Forum, 2021). In this new model, collaboration is enhanced, not just for unlocking innovations but also for supporting the well-being and safety of workers, customers, and local communities. These three pillars for the reset will unlock millions of dollars worldwide and boost what I call the *startup and multistakeholder economy,* driven by entrepreneurial minds.

A great example of this new model is the collaboration we've seen during the COVID-19 crisis to launch a new vaccine in a record time. "Companies, universities, and others have joined forces to develop diagnostics, therapeutics, and possible vaccines; establish testing centers; create mechanisms for tracing infections; and deliver telemedicine. Imagine what could be possible if similar concerted efforts were made in every sector" (Schwab, 2020).

Such collaboration will be happening more and more in the future, not only for vaccines but overcoming sustainability issues such as the world's damaging palm oil production or making transportation in cities safer and greener.

Overall, Joint Ventures (JVs) and partnerships are crucial to Innovation. In 2019, Airbus, Celanese, Engie, Vodafone, and Volkswagen relied on non-controlled JVs for more than 20 percent of their earnings, while at Coca-Cola, GM, and many others, that figure was above 10 percent (Bamford, Baynham, and Ernst, 2020).

However, often those corporate alliances fail—60 to 70 percent do not work. This is mainly because companies and people do not emphasize the right things. They suggest focusing less on the right business arrangement and more on developing the right working relationships. Also, they insist business leaders should not be concentrating on formal governance systems and structures but rather on enabling collaborative behavior (Hughes and Weiss, 2007).

We know everybody is motivated by different priorities, ideas, and values. This is why it is so challenging to work on significant problems together. We need a new type of mindset in the workplace to enable collaborative behavior, and this is where my book comes in. For that new model to work, the essential element will be trust. It will be the glue of our society, and I hope the seven mindset principles I shared will enable this.

IT STARTS WITH BELIEVING YOU CAN

Back in 2008, I didn't believe I could do anything to create an impact. I didn't think making an impact was within my reach, so I wouldn't even have tried it.

I always thought, *Why do I need to suffer? Why can't I just have fun and have an enjoyable life?* I was about to turn fifteen, and a significant life milestone came. In the school system in France, everyone undergoes primary education named "*le collège*" until the age of fifteen. After that, one can choose to either go for an apprenticeship, go to high school, continue with a manual school (a school to develop skills in using the hands and to teach practical arts such as woodworking, metalworking, and so on). In France, most kids go to high school. As you can imagine, everyone started to ask me, "What do you want to do later, Mikel?"

At that time, I wanted to be a waiter, then an electrician...or maybe a cabinet maker. I was overwhelmed. I didn't care about school and had no ambition for an academic career back then. Somehow, I started to be surrounded by people with a definite educational purpose, including my girlfriend at the time, who was first in her class.

In September 2008, I finally joined the high school in the city nearby. Despite my poor grades, my mom convinced the teachers to let me go there. Since one of the classes wasn't complete, there was a spot open for me. When I started high school, I was afraid. I was in a class with new people, in a new city, with new teachers. None of my friends were with me. Being lost in this new environment was my life crisis. I remember saying to myself, "What the hell am I doing here?" In time, I started surrounding myself with disciplined people who worked hard to get good grades—and they were fun. They became my best friends, and I started performing well at school. Also, my chemistry teacher made science sound so simple. He was passionate about science and talked about the world's most significant discoveries and scientists—Galileo, Einstein, Mendeleev. Fast forward ten years and I'm graduating from the University of Freiburg in Germany with a master's degree in chemistry.

During my chemistry studies, I always enjoyed learning about the journey of those innovators: Galileo, Einstein, Edison, etc. I thought about what these scientists or the world's greatest innovators, change-makers, had in common. I believe it's this:

- They were all life-long learners
- They were all patient
- They were extremely curious and asked many questions to detect the underlying *why* of anything they were studying

- They all challenged common assumptions; some even went to jail for it
- They were all courageous to fight against the odds

Their names are familiar to us today because they proved to be right. By convincing the masses, they impacted billions.

This book started with Carl Djerassi, who developed the birth control pill. His experiences highlight the message of my book. Connect previously unrelated dots, meet people, try and experiment, fail, embrace interdisciplinarity, and learn from everyone: science, art, history. The same message can be found in my favorite book, *The Alchemist*. Never stop chasing the opportunities that will enable you to change the world for the better. Those opportunities do not magically appear. Change your environment to discover better opportunities.

As a teenager, all I wanted was to enjoy life and have fun when I grew up. Today, I am committed to having a lasting impact on the world, experiencing the power and fulfillment of pursuing a purposeful life. Anyone living a life of purpose will go through ups and downs, encountering many uncomfortable moments of rejection. However, your purpose will be a never-ending source of fuel for your life.

THE FUTURE BELONGS TO THE ONES SEEKING PURPOSE

A few years ago, I connected with Harold Sinnott. Harold is a digital marketing consultant and ranked as a top influencer in digital transformation, emerging technologies, future of work, and business intelligence. Before becoming a consultant, he worked as a human resources director at several prominent companies, such as Citi, Telefonica, Motorola, DHL, and Johnson & Johnson. Harold has a ton of experience in work culture and what makes businesses successful.

"We talk about technology, and it's very important to discuss the technical aspects of technology. But we need to start with purpose and values because that determines how and what we do," mentioned Harold. Since childhood, he has tried to understand why different cultures behave differently. And so, in whatever he does today in his personal life or his career, he identifies the purpose and values of his actions. So should everybody.

No matter what we do, identifying the purpose should come first. You will be more fulfilled, your ROI will be higher, you will find it easier to build networks, and your impact on the world will be much more significant.

It starts with the new generation. Young people want to join purposeful companies. The Deloitte Millennial Survey from 2014 highlighted that more than 70 percent of Millennials expect their employers to focus on societal or mission-driven problems. When a company focuses on these, it's a purpose-driven company millennials want to work for.

According to the *Deloitte Review* article, "Becoming Irresistible: A New Model for Employee Engagement," mission-driven companies have 30 percent higher levels of innovation and 40 percent higher levels of employee retention.

An eight-year study of high-growth companies looked for traditional drivers behind success, such as innovation. It found that purpose created more unified organizations, more-motivated stakeholders, and more profitable growth (Malnight, Buche, and Dhanaraj, 2019).

You've probably seen Simon Sinek's 2009 TEDx Talk, "How Great Leaders Inspire Action," wherein he discusses the core topics of his book, *The Power of Why*. His talks, books, and messages are still impacting millions of lives worldwide—for a good reason. More and more of us want to be understood, and a company saying, "We will make a ton of profit," won't attract the best talent anymore. As Simon so insightfully points out, "One hundred percent of employees are people. One hundred percent of customers are people. One hundred percent of investors are people. If you don't understand people, you don't understand business."

This quote and the quote from Peter Drucker at the beginning of this chapter capture the essence: you can't run a company for the sake of profits. It's about the value and impact you generate in the world. A new generation of human beings wishes to make this world better. These people want to be more. These people want to be fulfilled. Passion is about finding yourself; purpose is about losing yourself in something bigger than you. Life should be about wanting to make a difference, help, give and serve.

It is an incredible time to be alive. The beauty of today's world is, with the availability of digital technologies and the new economic setup we're about to experience, absolutely everyone can be part of a positive change and make a difference.

MINDSET AND NETWORKS TO BOOST INNOVATION AND CHANGE

My biggest inspiration for writing this book was living in and meeting the people of Silicon Valley and seeing what they are doing differently. They evolve and succeed as a network. As Greg Satell, an expert in global transformation and change, whom I mentioned in Chapter 7, puts it, "The reality of today's world is that connection wins and isolation loses." Greg highlights this culture of openness and meritocracy has made Silicon Valley an ideal place for the immigrant to thrive. Everyone is included. As AnnaLee Saxenian said in an interview with Greg, "Everybody worked for the same company—Silicon Valley. (Satell, 2019)

In my search to understand why Silicon Valley was so different, I came across many books written on this topic. AnnaLee Saxenian's first book, *Regional Advantage: Culture and Competition in Silicon Valley and Route 128*, chronicles how Silicon Valley's network-driven economy propelled it past Boston's more hierarchical structure in the 1980s. Her subsequent book, *The New Argonauts: Regional Advantage in a Global Economy*, explains how Silicon Valley became a global phenomenon. Then there's *The Rainforest: The Secret to Building the Next Silicon Valley* by Victor Hwang and Greg Horowitt. These books emphasize the importance of human networks that generate extraordinary creativity and output.

To sum it up, Greg Satell points out the informal ties among entrepreneurs make new technology centers thrive. That's what makes Silicon Valley so successful. It's the network. It's about the people.

While some of my European colleagues might object with sentiments like, "This is too American," we need more of this mindset in Europe. In Germany, for instance, too few people decide to start companies. Only 5 percent of the population have plans to start a company. Experts give two reasons for this. The first is a lack of an entrepreneurial mindset. Second is the obstacles in the funding process, such as the fear of financial insecurity or the absence of entrepreneurial knowledge. (Berger-de Leon et al., 2021).

The most innovative places in the world have a prominent common denominator: networking and the mindset of sharing and working as a community.

Gernot Hutter, Ph.D., is the founder and manager of the innovation agency N17, which focuses on sustainability and communication. Previously he also co-founded the *Institut für Intrapreneurship*, a consulting company helping companies to train employees to become intrapreneurs. He says:

"In my last meeting with an innovation expert from Israel, I learned that their corporates were willing to share their know-how and ideas, so to say, as a second source of innovation aside from startups in this ecosystem. And that impressed me very much as this is impossible here in the DACH world, in the German-speaking countries. So, a strong ecosystem is, of course, the ideal basis for transformative innovation—and inside this ecosystem, the shared power of creativity boosts transformative innovation."

Money, tools, education, cash—these are not enough. We need a behavior change to enable a culture of trust openness to unleash transformative innovation.

For me, creating change in the multistakeholder economy is about harnessing the power of networks. However, not everyone can leverage the opportunity. To create, join, or grow a network for maximum change, you have to start with your mindset. In this book, I presented seven mindset principles to build, join, and leverage the power of networks, inspired by personal interviews and experiences, and research from change-makers.

- Mindset Principle 1—DO-IT-YOURSELF, Take Ownership
- Mindset Principle 2—Blow Up Borders
- Mindset Principle 3—Be of Value. Give Before You Get
- Mindset Principle 4—Start Small, Grow Big, with Purpose
- Mindset Principle 5—Do What You Can't
- Mindset Principle 6—Go Viral
- Mindset Principle 7—Be Bold, and Have Skin in The Game

There is a huge advantage to using them. You will build your networks and gain access to:

- Knowledge and ideas: This will enhance your creativity and help you build complex concepts; you will have access to insights, technologies, stories, and educational content.
- Resources: You will attract the capital you need, such as revenue, debt, equity, grant financing, or access to the proper infrastructure for your dream company: a happy

place where you established a great culture, which will help your idea grow. Access to marketing opportunities, databases containing critical data, and more.

- People: You will create the right culture by attracting the best talent with the right set of skills, experience, diversity, and knowledge. The people with the right mindset, behaviors, inclusiveness, and love of the place you dream about.

To conclude this book, I would like to finish with a description of the workplace and way of life many of us will experience.

THE WORKPLACE OF THE FUTURE

What are we about to experience in the coming years? As Jacob Morgan puts it, "Work as we know it is dead, and the only way forward is to challenge convention around how we work, how we lead, and how we build our companies." I can't agree more! (Morgan, 2014)

Jacob Morgan is a futurist, keynote speaker, and multiple best-selling author, including *The Future Leader: 9 Skills and Mindsets to Succeed in the Next Decade*. He describes how employees are evolving and organizations, as a consequence, must not only embrace this evolution but prepare for and encourage it (Morgan, 2014). While Jacob originally described this in 2014, the COVID-19 pandemic accelerated the trend, coming faster than we think. The ones at the center of networks, proactively building and growing them, will thrive in this new world.

Employees in the Past	Employees in the Future
• Work nine to five	• Work anytime
• Work in a corporate office	• Work anywhere
• Use company equipment	• Use any device
• Focused on inputs	• Focused on outputs
• Climb the corporate ladder	• Create your own ladder
• Pre-defined work	• Customized work
• Hoards information	• Shares information
• No voice	• Can become a leader
• Relies on email	• Relies on collaboration technologies
• Focused on knowledge	• Focus on adaptive learning
• Corporate learning and teaching	• Democratized learning and teaching

Change is necessary. Everything in our society will continue to evolve as networks, and this is precisely where the opportunity lies. Those able to leverage the power will have the most significant positive impact on society.

REACH OUT TO ME

I would love to hear from you. If you have questions, remarks, or would like to engage further on the topic, feel free to reach out to me or tag me on LinkedIn, where I am the most active (@Mikel Mangold) or on Instagram (@mikelmangold). You can also write to me at mikel.mangold@gmail.com.

PS: Can you do me a favor? It's a small one, but it will mean the world to me. Would you write a review of this book on

Amazon? While it will only take you a few minutes, the credibility that your rating brings will help spread my message and make a positive impact on people's lives. Thank you!

Acknowledgments

In creating this book, I had the opportunity to interview many different people—generalists and world experts—within the startup, innovation, change management, and investments industry. Thank you for taking the time out of your busy schedules to share what you know with me and the world, and thank you for guiding me toward the best studies. Each conversation was an incredible lesson and made me curious to learn more. Without you, this book would not have become a reality.

This book is also for all the people who have mentored me, coached me, and given me my first opportunities long before everyone else did: Clément Roux, Franck Velikonia, Eric Guerra, Serge Neunlist, Carole Fuchs, Laurine Schmidlin, Sven Küspert, Dirk Schapeler, Rama Penta, Christopher Haskell, Nina Luu, Diana Joseph, Susan Windham-Bannister, Eylem Demir Sentürk, Ganzo-San, Frank Kumli, and the 205-plus backers who invested in me and this book before it was real. Without their support, I would not have made it to where I am now.

Lastly, this book was made possible also by a community of beta readers who reviewed my chapters upfront and provided me with sincere and constructive feedback. A special thanks to Mayur Gaikwad, Manuelle Backer, Jean-Raymond Raymond, Cathy Zhang, Gian Nutal Schädli, Patty Sherin, Pauline Maurer, Birgit Fuhrmann, Fabiola Fajardo Fregoso, Marjorie Gomez, Matt Müller, Simon Vanhoucke, and Léo Edel, who reviewed many chapters and spent hours reading them. A big shoutout to my marketing and revisions editor, Jacques, with whom I spent months working together.

Nearly everyone is "too busy," but some are making the time because they care. I will be forever grateful to all the people who took the time. You are unique, and as promised, the name of all my backers and people involved with the book (listed in alphabetical order by the first name).

Abe Janis	Axel Schultze
Alana Dixson	Beat Meyer
Alex Antebi	Benedicte Chouik
Alexandra Böhringer	Beyza Gizem Arikan
Alice Bosley	Bhagyashree Deokar
Alyssa Wengi	Birgit Fuhrmann
Amy Abdelhalim	Blaise Jacholkowski
Angela Laffan	Bojan Davinic
Angèle Aubry	Julien Bossard
Anna-Lena Lorenz	Brad Feld
Anne-Schönfließ	Brenda Ziegler
Antoine Frayssinet	Brijen Patel
Antoine Koerckel	Carole Fuchs
Ashish Pattanayak	Carsten Dietrich
Asli Tuncag	Catherine Mangold

Catherine Rey
Cathy Zhang
Cecilia Aiello
Cécilia Guerin
Charlene Li
Charles J Costa
Charlotte Singerholm Gert Hansen
Christelle Wolff
Christina Kumar
Christina Nesheva
Christine Johrend
Christine Simon
Christof Matt
Christopher A. Haskell
Cimin Wirth
Claire Maurer
Clément Roux
Clement Segal
Corinne Mangold
Cristian Marie Lopez
Cyril Aubry
David Giltner
Debra De Silva-Sun
Deepti Pahwa
Diana Joseph
Dino Husejnagic
Diogo Magalhães e Silva
Dirk Schapeler
Dominik Bischoff
Dr. Birk Stange
Dustin Kubas

Duy Quoc Le Nguyen
Elena Perju
Elyes Bouzizoua
Emmanuel Retournard
Emmanuel Rey
Eric Koester
Eric Quon-Lee
Erick Romero
Eva-Maria Krauel
Eylem Demir Sentürk
Fabio Molina Bueno
Fabiola Fajardo Fregoso
Florence Cotillon
Florent Buschiazzo
Florenz Unold
Florian Köpfer
Fluhr Florian
Francesco
François Wolff
Frank Kumli
Franz Graeter
G. Kofi Annan
Gabriele Mangold
Gernot Hutter
Gerold Manthey
Gerrit Schoettler
Gian Nutal Schädli
Glenn Davis
Greg Satell
Harold Sinnott
Hatice Zehra Doğru
Ian Hathaway

Jacky Mangold

Jacqueline Mangold

Jan Engels

Jan Stieler

Jan-Philipp Kruse

Janice Fong Hansen

Jaochim Dietrich

Jasmien De Ryck

Jay Wadia

Jaykant Patel

Jean-Pierre Champel

Jean-Raymond Naveau

Jennielyn Dino Rossi

Jocelyn Toll

Jochen Berbuer

Joel Patel

John Tompkins

Johny Decroix

Jordy Mansuy

Joshua Littlejohn

Jousson Catherine

Ju Du

Jules Hoernle

Karim Vadiwala

Karin Müller

Kiliana Suzart-Woischnik

Lars Behrendt

Lars Munter

Lauren Brown

Laurence Jacob

Lauriane Cotter

Laurine Schmidlin

Lea-Marie Mangold

Lee Towe

Léo Edel

Linda Zafra

Lisa Feiler

Lisa Rothstein

Manak Shah

Manon Claden

Manuelle Backer

Mariana Piovezani Moreti

Marie-Ange Fels

Marion Herdlicka

Marjorie Gomez

Mark Koester

Marko Katajisto

Marta Jakab

Martina Truche

Matt Mueller

Mayur Gaikwad

Mikel Kauffmann

Milena Stoycheva

Mohamed Hashim Omer

Monica Moldovan

Monique Wright

Nadine Champel

Naveen Jain

Nicolas Das Neves

Nicolas Gebel

Nicolas Schmitt

Nicolas Schneider

Nicole H. Romano

Nicole Medina

Nina Luu
Noteh Krauss
Olga Kagan
Olivier Staub
Pamela Lisboa
Pan Baihan
Patricia Letayf
Patty Sherin
Paul Coyle
Pauline Maurer
Percy Grunwald
Philippe Méresse
Rama K. Penta
Regina Gripenberg
Remy Bailly
Renee Williams
Ricardo Hurmus
Richard Hughes
Richard Wu
Robert Alan Mansfield
Robin Taylor
Romaric Corsi
Rosen Dimitrov
Sandrine Hell
Sarah Muller
Sarah Richard
Sarah Simon
Sasa Spasic
Sathya La Bolle
Sayeh Beiglari
Selim Salman
Serge Neunlist

Serge Simon
Shane Neblett
Simon Maechling
Simon Nopp
Simon Paillaud
Simon Plovyt
Simon Rey
Simon Vanhoucke
Simran Arora
Solange Massa
Soulaimane Zariouh
Stefan Dietrich
Stefan Schwarz
Stephanie Jaalouk
Stephanie Thoma
Stephen Parkins
Steve Rommel
Stuart Gregg
Susan Windham-Bannister
Sven Knüspert
Tabea Bicalho-Nagel
Tatjana Gust
Thaís Moreira
Théo Champel
Thierry Mangold
Thoma Kindbeiter
Thomas Herget
Tony Namulo
Uwe Zell
Vasiliki Anest
Veronica Dodero
Veronica Lobkina

Vipul Swamy Ballupet
Virgile Allonas
Virginie Goetz
Win Phyo
Yacine Cherraoui
Yannick Mangold
Yasmine Gagou
Yauhen Sheima
Yvonne Stender
Zheni Mio

I would like to recognize everyone else who is not mentioned in my acknowledgments but who still shaped the way I think and behave, which helped me build the narrative and message of this book and my life.

Appendix

INTRODUCTION

Annual Reviews. "A Conversation with Carl Djerassi." April 13, 2012. Video, 1:11:57, https://youtu.be/OVL8FKitRLM.

Anthony, Scott D., S. Patrick Viguerie, and Andrew Waldeck. *Corporate Longevity: Turbulence Ahead for Large Organizations.* Innosight, 2016. https://www.innosight.com/wp-content/uploads/2016/08/Corporate-Longevity-2016-Final.pdf.

Baroudy, Kim, Jonatan Janmark, Tobias Strålin, Abhi Satyavarapu, and Zeno Ziemke "Europe's Startup Ecosystem: Heating Up, but Still Facing Challenges." *McKinsey & Company.* Last updated October 11, 2020. https://www.mckinsey.com/industries/technology-media-and-telecommunications/our-insights/europes-startup-ecosystem-heating-up-but-still-facing-challenges.

Bonchek, Mark. "How to Create an Exponential Mindset" *Harvard Business Review,* July 27, 2016. https://hbr.org/2016/07/how-to-create-an-exponential-mindset.

Corbyn, Zoë. "Peter Diamandis: 'In the next 10 years, we'll reinvent every industry'." *The Guardian*, January 25, 2020. https://www.theguardian.com/technology/2020/jan/25/peter-diamandis-future-faster-think-interview-ai-industry.

Hagel, John, John Seely Brown, Maggie Wooll, and Alok Ranjan. "If You Love Them, Set Them Free." *Deloitte Insights*. Last modified June 6, 2017. https://www2.deloitte.com/us/en/insights/topics/talent/future-workforce-engagement-in-the-workplace.html.

Harding, Charlotte. "Young People Losing Hope of Achieving Future Dreams Due to Pandemic." *SussexWorld*, October 27, 2020. https://www.brightonandhoveindependent.co.uk/news/people/young-people-losing-hope-achieving-future-dreams-due-pandemic-3016428.

Macmillan Dictionary. s.v. "Wantrepreneurs." Accessed September 12, 2021. https://www.macmillandictionary.com/dictionary/british/wantrepreneur.

McKinsey & Company. *Building the European Biotech Sector with Science and Innovation*. Last modified August 5, 2021. https://www.mckinsey.com/industries/life-sciences/our-insights/infographic-building-the-european-biotech-sector-with-world-class-science-and-innovation.

Osterwalder, Alexander, Tendayi Viki, and Yves Pigneur. "Why Your Organization Needs an Innovation Ecosystem." *Harvard Business Review*, November 15, 2019. https://hbr.org/2019/11/why-your-organization-needs-an-innovation-ecosystem.

Performance: Accelerated, A New Benchmark for Initiating Employee Engagement, Retention and Results. Salt Lake City, UT: O.C. Tanner Learning Group, n.d. https://www.octanner.com/content/dam/oc-tanner/documents/global-research/White_Paper_Performance_Accelerated.pdf.

Sneader, Kevin, and Shubham Singhal. "The Next Normal Arrives: Trends for 2021." *McKinsey & Company.* January 4, 2021. https://www.mckinsey.com/featured-insights/leadership/the-next-normal-arrives-trends-that-will-define-2021-and-beyond.

Tharoor, Ishaan. "The 'Great Resignation' goes global." The Washington Post, October 18, 2021. https://www.washingtonpost.com/world/2021/10/18/labor-great-resignation-global/.

Unold, Florenz. "Development of a Visual Tool to Design and Assess Operating Models for Corporate Idea and Innovation Management (I^{2}M)." (master's thesis, Goethe University Frankfurt, 2021).

World Health Organization (WHO). "1 in 3 People Globally Do Not Have Access to Safe Drinking Water—UNICEF, WHO." World Health Organization press release, June 18, 2019. World Health Organization website. https://www.who.int/news/item/18-06-2019-1-in-3-people-globally-do-not-have-access-to-safe-drinking-water-unicef-who.

CHAPTER 1

Alderman, Liz. "Macron Vowed to Make France a 'Startup Nation.' Is It Getting There?" *New York Times*, May 23, 2018. https://

www.nytimes.com/2018/05/23/business/emmanuel-macron-france-technology.html.

Bower, Joseph L. and Clayton M. Christensen. "Disruptive Technologies: Catching the Wave." *Harvard Business Review*, January–February 1995. https://hbr.org/1995/01/disruptive-technologies-catching-the-wave.

Chong, Alvin. "In-depth: Time Consciousness and Discipline in the Industrial Revolution: The story of how time came to govern the industry, and then life." *SJX Watches. Last modified* July 21, 2020. https://watchesbysjx.com/2020/07/time-consciousness-and-discipline-industrial-revolution.html.

Engel, Jacob M. "Why Does Culture 'Eat Strategy for Breakfast'?" *Forbes,* November 20, 2018. https://www.forbes.com/sites/forbescoachescouncil/2018/11/20/why-does-culture-eat-strategy-for-breakfast/.

Feld, Brad, and Ian Hathaway. *The Startup Community Way: Evolving an Entrepreneurial Ecosystem.* Hoboken, New Jersey: John Wiley & Sons, 2020.

Geilinger, Ulrich, and Chandra Leo. *HBM New Drug Approval Report: Analysis of FDA New Drug Approvals in 2018 (and Multi-Year Trends).* Zug, Switzerland: HBM Partners, 2019.

Hollinger, Peggy, Donato Paolo Mancini, and Andrew Jack "Roche Boss Who Says Bitter Pill of Truth Is Only Way to Build Trust." *SWI swissinfo.ch,* April 25, 2020. https://www.swissinfo.ch/eng/pharma_roche-boss-who-says-bitter-pill-of-truth-is-only-way-to-build-trust-/45715996.

IGI Global. *What is Exponential Technology.* Accessed January 8th, 2021. https://www.igi-global.com/dictionary/exponential-technology/73515.

Joseph, Diana, Susan Windham-Bannister, and Mikel Mangold. "What Corporates Can Do to Help an Innovation Ecosystem Thrive-and Why They Should Do It." *Journal of Commercial Biotechnology* 26, no. 1 (March 16, 2021). https://doi.org/10.5912/jcb975.

Leuty, Ron. "40 Years After Genentech Set Biotech Industry Standards, Is It Still Disruptive–Or Disrupted?" *San Francisco Business Times*, May 20, 2016. https://www.bizjournals.com/sanfrancisco/print-edition/2016/05/20/genentech-biotech-roche-goeddel-levinson-scheller.html.

McKinsey & Company. "Deutsche Gründerlandschaft kann 1,4 Millionen neue Jobs bis 2030 schaffen." McKinsey & Company press release, October 26, 2021. McKinsey & Company website. https://www.mckinsey.de/news/presse/perspektive-start-up-ecosystem-gruenderlandschaft-deutschland-2030.

Polman, Paul, and Andrew Winston. *Net Positive: How Courageous Companies Thrive by Giving More Than They Take.* Boston: Harvard Business Review Press, 2021.

Prosser, Daniel F. *Thirteeners: Why Only 13 Percent of Companies Successfully Execute Their Strategy—and How Yours Can Be One of Them.* Austin: Greenleaf Book Group Press, 2015.

Razzetti, Gustavo "How to Stop Living Life on Autopilot." *The Adaptive Mind* (blog). *Psychology Today.* November 1, 2018. https://www.psychologytoday.com/us/blog/the-adaptive-mind/201811/how-stop-living-life-autopilot.

Reynolds, Jonathan (@Jonathan Reynolds). "Great cartoon! Ultimately there is no choice, as change is going to happen whether we want it to or not... it is after all the very fabric of reality." Comment on @Mikelmangold. Linkedin, 2021.

https://www.linkedin.com/feed/update/urn:li:activity:6801068971123605506?commentUrn=urn%3Ali%3A-comment%3A%28activity%3A6801068971123605506%2C6801950197942505472%29.

Strategy&. "2018 Global Innovation 1000 Study: What the Top Innovators Get Right". October 29, 2018. Video, 2:36. https://youtu.be/yHWEvywQNe4.

Terwilliger, Jay. "The Three Levels of Innovation." *The Innovation Blog. Creative Realities*, September 30, 2015.

Thompson, Neil, Didier Bonnet, and Sarah Jaballah. *Lifting the Lid on Corporate Innovation in the Digital Age.* Paris: Capgemini, 2020. https://www.capgemini.com/wp-content/uploads/2020/05/MIT-INVENT-Report_NEW-2020.pdf.

CHAPTER 2

Agile Radicals (blog). "The Spotify Model (2/2)," September 21, 2020. https://agile-radicals.de/en/the-spotify-model-2-2.

Collins, Randall. *The Sociology of Philosophies: A Global Theory of Intellectual Change.* Cambridge, Massachusetts: Harvard University Press, 1998.

Concilio, Grazia, Chuan Li, Pau Rausell, and Ilaria Tosoni. "Cities as Enablers of Innovation." In *Innovation Capacity and the City,* edited by Grazia Concilio and Ilaria Tosoni, 43-60. New York, NY: Springer, 2018.

Feld, Brad, and Ian Hathaway. *The Startup Community Way: Evolving an Entrepreneurial Ecosystem.* Hoboken, New Jersey: John Wiley & Sons. 2020.

Fricker, Mark D., Luke L. M. Heaton, Nick S. Jones, and Lynne Boddy. "The Mycelium as a Network." In *The Fungal Kingdom,* edited by Joseph Heitman, Barbara J. Howlett, Pedro W. Crous, Eva H. Stukenbrock, Timothy Y. James, and Neil A. R. Gow 335-367. Washington, DC: ASM Press, 2017.

Herry, Cyril, Dominik R. Bach, Fabrizio Esposito, Francesco Di Salle, Walter J Perrig, Klaus Scheffler, Andreas Lüthi, and Erich Seifritz. "Processing of Temporal Unpredictability in the Human and Animal Amygdala." *The Journal of Neuroscience* 27, no. 22 (May 30, 2007): 5958-66.

Ishak, Waguih. "Creating an Innovation Culture." *McKinsey & Company.* Last modified September 28, 2017. https://www.mckinsey.com/business-functions/strategy-and-corporate-finance/our-insights/creating-an-innovation-culture.

Johnson, Steven. *Where Good Ideas Come From: The Seven Patterns of Innovation.* London, England: Penguin Random House, 2011.

Kahneman, Daniel. *Thinking, Fast and Slow.* New York: Farrar, Straus, and Giroux. 2017.

Nir and Far. *Exactly What Is Motivation? Surprisingly, Not What You Think.* Accessed February 23, 2022. https://www.nirandfar.com/what-is-motivation/.

Page, Scott E. *The Diversity Bonus: How Great Teams Pay Off in the Knowledge Economy.* Princeton, NJ: Princeton University Press, 2017.

Rigby, Darrell K., Jeff Sutherland, and Andy Noble. "Agile at Scale." *Harvard Business Review,* May-June 2018. https://hbr.org/2018/05/agile-at-scale.

Weiss, Rick. "Researchers Go from A to B to Discovery." *Washington Post,* January 26, 1998. https://www.washingtonpost.com/wp-srv/national/science/jan98/discovery26.htm.

Monumental Trees. *General Sherman, the Biggest Tree in the World.* Accessed February 23, 2022. https://www.monumentaltrees.com/en/trees/giantsequoia/biggest_tree_in_the_world/.

CHAPTER 3

Global Startup Ecosystem Index. Tel Aviv: StartupBlink, 2021. https://www.startupblink.com/startupecosystemreport.pdf.

Jain, Naveen. "The Power of Boldness." Mindvalley online course, January 2021. https://www.mindvalley.com/boldness.

Merriam-Webster. s.v. "moonshot." Accessed January 10, 2022. https://www.merriam-webster.com/dictionary/moonshot.

Mikel Mangold. "Ep 5. #Bioimpact Silicon Valley: Systems, Maps & Education with Gregory Theyel." January 21, 2021. Video, 35:34. https://youtu.be/JThDi7bgQrI.

Peter H. Diamandis, MD (@PeterDiamandis). "Peter's Law #22: The Day before Something Is a Breakthrough, It's a Crazy Idea." Twitter, December 24, 2012. https://twitter.com/PeterDiamandis/status/283196701794250752?s=20.

Pulkkinen, Levi. "If Silicon Valley Were a Country, It Would Be among the Richest on Earth." *The Guardian*, April 30, 2019. https://www.theguardian.com/technology/2019/apr/30/silicon-valley-wealth-second-richest-country-world-earth.

CHAPTER 4

Ceci, Laura. "Apple App Store: Annual Gross App Revenue 2017-2021." *Statistica*. December 13, 2021. https://www.statista.com/statistics/296226/annual-apple-app-store-revenue/.

Erlichman, Jon (@JonErlichman). "Apple's App Store revenue: 2020: $72 billion 2019: $56 billion 2018: $47 billion 2017: $39 billion 2016: $29 billion 2015: $20 billion 2014: $15 billion 2013." Twitter, November 24, 2021. https://twitter.com/JonErlichman/status/1463599560362708998?s=20&t=oKrJXuAQNk7Yk5S_SDE65Q.

Feld, Brad, and Ian Hathaway. *The Startup Community Way: Evolving an Entrepreneurial Ecosystem.* Hoboken, New Jersey: John Wiley & Sons, 2020.

Goodreads. *Quote by Nelson Mandela: "There is no passion to be found playing small -...".* Accessed February 25, 2022. https://www.goodreads.com/quotes/49585-there-is-no-passion-to-be-found-playing-small--.

Grant, Adam. "Persuading the Unpersuadable." *Harvard Business Review,* March-April 2021. https://hbr.org/2021/03/persuading-the-unpersuadable.

Haudan, Jim. "Creating a Culture of Risk Taking—How Do We Risk Our Assets to Keep Growing, but Not Put Everything at Risk?" *Inc.com,* October 27, 2016. https://www.inc.com/jim-haudan/creating-a-culture-of-risk-taking.html.

Kirsner, Scott "The 10 Most Influential Women in Biotech." *The Boston Globe,* September 15, 2013. https://www.bostonglobe.com/business/2013/09/14/the-most-influential-women-biotech/gba2RTZ1SuJLt5a9wYwasO/story.html.

Margolis, Michael. *Story 10x: Turn the Impossible into the Inevitable.* Vancouver: Page Two, 2019.

Merchant, Brian. "The Secret Origin Story of the iPhone—An Exclusive Excerpt From *The One Device.*" *The Verge,* June 13, 2017. https://www.theverge.com/2017/6/13/15782200/one-device-secret-history-iphone-brian-merchant-book-excerpt.

Parrish, Charlie. "Meet The PayPal Mafia, The Richest Group of Men in Silicon Valley." *Business Insider,* September 20, 2014. https://www.businessinsider.com/meet-the-paypal-mafia-the-richest-group-of-men-in-silicon-valley-2014-9.

Razzetti, Gustavo "How to Stop Living Life on Autopilot." *The Adaptive Mind* (blog). *Psychology Today.* November 1, 2018. https://www.psychologytoday.com/us/blog/the-adaptive-mind/201811/how-stop-living-life-autopilot.

Stanford eCorner. "Reid Hoffman: Entrepreneurs Will Create the Future [Entire Talk]." July 07, 2011. Video, 42:56. https://youtu.be/tmNmOlx1w-A.

Wozniak, Steve. "Steve 'Woz' Wozniak - Creator Speaker Notes (Summer 2021)." Interview by Eric Koester. *Creator institute.* June 23, 2021. Video, 29:02.

CHAPTER 5

Belden Castonguay, Sharon. "The Psychology of Career Decisions." Filmed April 7, 2018 at TEDxWesleyanU, Middletown, CT. Video, 12:26. https://www.ted.com/talks/sharon_belden_castonguay_the_psychology_of_career_decisions.

Hagel, John, John Seely Brown, Maggie Wooll, and Alok Ranjan. "If You Love Them, Set Them Free." *Deloitte Insights*, June 6, 2017. https://www2.deloitte.com/global/en/insights/topics/talent/future-workforce-engagement-in-the-workplace.html.

Houston, Eric. "How Rats, Bats, Bees, and People Navigate Their Worlds." *Association for Psychological Science*, July 29, 2016.

https://www.psychologicalscience.org/observer/how-rats-bats-bees-and-people-navigate-their-worlds.

Maddux, William and A. D. Galinsky. "Cultural Borders and Mental Barriers: The Relationship Between Living Abroad and Creativity.," *Journal of Personality and Social Psychology* 96, no.5 (2009): 1047-61. https://doi.apa.org/doi/10.1037/a0014861.

Meakin, Lucy. "100 Million Workers May Need to Switch Occupation by 2030." *Bloomberg*, February 18, 2021. https://www.bloomberg.com/news/articles/2021-02-18/100-million-workers-may-need-to-switch-occupation-by-2030-chart.

Narasimhan, Vas, Jorge Conde, Vijay Pande, and Sonal Chokshi. "a16z Podcast: The Science and Business of Innovative Medicines." January 13, 2019. Podcast, MP3 audio, 59:02. https://a16z.com/2019/01/13/pharma-business-innovation-medicine-next-therapeutics/.

Nink, Marco. "Only 15% of Employees in Germany Are Engaged." *Gallup Business Journal*, July 1, 2015. Accessed February 19, 2022. https://news.gallup.com/businessjournal/183851/employees-germany-engaged.aspx.

Sorenson, Susan. "How Employee Engagement Drives Growth" *Gallup*. Last modified June 20, 2013. https://www.gallup.com/workplace/236927/employee-engagement-drives-growth.aspx.

Stanford. "Steve Jobs' 2005 Stanford Commencement Address." March 8, 2008. Video 15:04. https://youtu.be/UF8uR6Z6KLc.

Techstars. *Techstars Startup Weekend.* Accessed December 16, 2021. https://www.techstars.com/communities/startup-weekend.

Tolman, Edward C. "Cognitive Maps in Rats and Men." *Psychological Review* 55, no. 4 (1948): 189–208. https://doi.org/10.1037/h0061626.

Witters, Dan, and Sangeeta Agrawal. "Well-Being Enhances Benefits of Employee Engagement." *Gallup.* October 27, 2015. Accessed February 19, 2022. https://www.gallup.com/workplace/236483/enhances-benefits-employee-engagement.aspx.

CHAPTER 6

Caprino, Kathy. "Co-Elevation: How to Achieve Positive Leadership Impact Without Pre-Established Authority." *Forbes,* May 22, 2020. https://www.forbes.com/sites/kathycaprino/2020/05/22/co-elevation-how-to-achieve-positive-leadership-impact-without-pre-established-authority.

Co-Elevation. *Co-Elevation.* Accessed January 27, 2022. https://www.coelevation.com.

Cohen, David, and Brad Feld. "Give First with David Cohen and Brad Feld." *Techstars.* Accessed February 20, 2022. https://www.techstars.com/the-line/podcasts/give-first.

Edet, Nsikak (@nsikak edet). "Well, it's be months since we last had a chat. Just wanted you to know that before I messaged you last year on career advice as a young chemistry graduate." Comment on @Mikelmangold. LinkedIn, 2021. https://www.linkedin.com/feed/update/urn:li:activity:6649387698807275520?com-

mentUrn=urn%3Ali%3Acomment%3A%28activity%3A66493
87698807275520%2C6651155801669021696%29.

Feld, Brad, and Ian Hathaway. *The Startup Community Way: Evolving an Entrepreneurial Ecosystem*. Hoboken, New Jersey: John Wiley & Sons. 2020.

Grant, Adam. "In the Company of Givers and Takers." *Harvard Business Review*, April 2013. https://hbr.org/2013/04/in-the-company-of-givers-and-takers.

Knight Foundation. "Asset Management Industry Severely Lacking Diversity, New Knight Foundation Study Finds; Signals Untapped Opportunity For Investors." Last modified December 7, 2021. https://knightfoundation.org/press/releases/asset-management-industry-severely-lacking-diversity-new-knight-foundation-study-finds-signals-untapped-opportunity-for-investors/.

Maschmeyer, Carsten (@Carsten Marschmeyer). "Gerade bin ich auf Startup-Tour in den USA. Für mich ist die Bay Area (Silicon Valley und San Francisco) nicht nur eine Region, sondern ein Ort voll kreativer." LinkedIn, November 2021. https://www.linkedin.com/posts/carsten-maschmeyer_startups-usa-activity-6862073321454940162-fGG4.

Mindvalley. *Introducing Ultimate Leadership by Keith Ferrazzi*. Accessed, January 27, 2022. https://www.mindvalley.com/leadership.

Nickisch, Curt. "Leaders Who Get How to Give." *Harvard Business Review*, January 24, 2017. https://hbr.org/2017/01/leaders-who-get-how-to-give.

Podsakoff, Nathan P., Steven W. Whiting, Philip Podsakoff, and Brian D. Blume. "Individual- and Organizational-Level Consequences of Organizational Citizenship Behaviors: A Meta-Analysis." *Journal of Applied Psychology* 94, no. 1 (January 2019): 122–41.

Techstars. Code of Conduct. Accessed December 11, 2021. https://www.techstars.com/code-of-conduct.

Turczynski, Bart. "2021 HR Statistics: Job Search, Hiring, Recruiting & Interviews." *Career Blog. Zety,* April 14, 2021. https://zety.com/blog/hr-statistics.

CHAPTER 7

Collins, Randall. *The Sociology of Philosophies: A Global Theory of Intellectual Change.* Cambridge: Belknap Press, 2000.

Desjardins, Jeff. "How Long Does It Take to Hit 50 Million Users?" *Visualcapitalist.* June 8, 2018. https://www.visualcapitalist.com/how-long-does-it-take-to-hit-50-million-users/.

Lev-Ram, Michal, "For Adobe, Cloud Traction Leads to Record-High Stock Price." *Fortune,* June 18, 2014. https://fortune.com/2014/06/18/for-adobe-cloud-traction-leads-to-record-high-stock-price.

Li, Charlene. "How Disruptors Build Trust and Power." *Leading Disruption* (blog). *LinkedIn*, June 7, 2021. https://www.linkedin.com/pulse/how-disruptors-build-trust-power-charlene-li.

Li, Charlene. *The Disruption Mindset: Why Some Organizations Transform While Others Fail.* Oakton: IdeaPress Publishing, 2019.

McLeod, Saul. "Asch Conformity Experiment." *Simply Psychology.* Last modified December 28, 2018. https://www.simplypsychology.org/asch-conformity.html.

Satell, Greg. "You Don't Need a Grand Strategy to Achieve Organizational Change." *Harvard Business Review,* March 10, 2020. https://hbr.org/2020/03/you-dont-need-a-grand-strategy-to-achieve-organizational-change.

Uzzi, Brian, Satyam Mukherjee, Michael Stringer, and Ben Jones. "Atypical Combinations and Scientific Impact." *Science* 342, no. 6157 (October 2013): 468-472. https://doi.org/10.1126/science.1240474.

CHAPTER 8

Diamandis, Peter. H. "How to Change Your Mindset: Peter's Laws Peter H. Diamandis." *Awaken.* May 18, 2013. https://awaken.com/2013/05/how-to-change-your-mindset-peters-laws/.

Five One Labs. *Five One Labs.* Accessed February 2, 2022. https://fiveonelabs.org.

Lakhiani, Vishen. "Which 'Brules' Are Holding You Back?" *Mindvalley Blog*. July 11, 2018. https://blog.mindvalley.com/vishen-lakhiani-brules/.

Peter H. Diamandis LLC. "Peter Diamandis." Speaking. https://www.diamandis.com/speaking.

Startup Columbia. "Alice Bosley '17 SIPA and Patricia Letayf '17 SIPA Entrepreneurs of the Year, Five One Labs, Co-Founders, Executive Director and Director of Operations." Accessed February 22, 2021. https://www.startupcolumbia.org/speakers/alice-bosley-17sipa-and-patricia-letayf-17-sipa.

SUCCESS Academy. "28 Uncommon Rules to Live By, From a Space Tech Billionaire" *SUCCESS Magazine*, May 24, 2016. https://www.success.com/28-uncommon-rules-to-live-by-from-a-space-tech-billionaire/.

TEDx Talks. "The art of innovation | Guy Kawasaki | TEDxBerkeley." February 23, 2014. Video, 21:15. https://youtu.be/Mtjatz9r-Vc.

Winspire Magazine. "The Story of Free Bagels by Simon Sinek - Winspire Magazine." April 6, 2017. Video, 2:20. https://youtu.be/K-E_KFDWMog.

CHAPTER 9

ChemicalWorldTour. "Le labo du futur - BAYER" February 24, 2017. Video, 7:34. https://youtu.be/4qFc6OdlvtM.

Holston, Mike (@therealtarzann). "This is who we fight for...they are losing the war against us...we must fight for them by any means necessary! Whatever it takes." Instagram, June 4th, 2021. https://www.instagram.com/p/CPs5gdlHcWe.

Ighirri, Alexia. "Alsace: Quand Un Étudiant Se Donne Pour Mission de Vulgariser la Chimie." *20 Minutes,* March 23, 2017. https://www.20minutes.fr/strasbourg/2028479-20170310-alsace-quand-etudiant-donne-mission-vulgariser-chimie.

Lakhiani, Vishen (a) (@Mindvalley) "Is this the greatest marketing mislead since big tobacco? It's up to us all to stand for our health and say NO to companies peddling dangerous products." Facebook, Video, February 24, 2020. https://fb.watch/b6dCmRo1gj.

Lakhiani, Vishen (b) (@Vishen) "I wanted to show you first hand some of the marketing traps and misleading labelling of 'healthy' products you consume every single day." Facebook, Video, January 25, 2020. https://fb.watch/b6dQvPlpEU.

Miller, Jason. "The Amazing Multiple Benefits When an Employee Shares Content". *Marketing Blog. LinkedIn.* January 31, 2017. https://www.linkedin.com/business/marketing/blog/content-marketing/the-amazing-multiple-benefits-when-an-employee-shares-content.

Ortiz-Ospina, Esteban. "The Rise of Social Media." *Our World in Data.* Last Modified, September 18, 2019. Accessed February 10, 2022. https://ourworldindata.org/rise-of-social-media.

CHAPTER 10

Badziag, Rafael. "Billionaire Who Made His First $1 Million at Microsoft: 'Bill Gates Was an Extremely Intense Person.'" *CNBC*, November 13, 2019. https://www.cnbc.com/2019/11/13/billionaire-and-ex-microsoft-employee-on-what-it-was-like-working-with-bill-gates.html.

Carson, Shelley. *Your Creative Brain: Seven Steps to Maximize Imagination, Productivity, and Innovation in Your Life.* Hoboken: Jossey-Bass Professional Learning, 2010.

Dyer, Jeff and Hal Gregersen. "Learn How to Think Different(ly)." *Harvard Business Review*, September 27, 2011. https://hbr.org/2011/09/begin-to-think-differently.

Gladwell, Malcolm. *Outliers: The Story of Success.* Back Bay Books: New York, 2011.

Piotr, Harry. "Apple - Think Different - Full Version." September 30, 2013. Video, 1:09. https://youtu.be/5sMBhDv4sik.

CHAPTER 11

Bamford, James, Gerard Baynham, and David Ernst. "Joint Ventures and Partnerships in a Downturn." *Harvard Business Review*, September-October 2020. https://hbr.org/2020/09/joint-ventures-and-partnerships-in-a-downturn.

"Becoming Irresistible: A New Model for Employee Engagement." *Deloitte Review*, January 27, 2015. https://www2.deloitte.com/us/en/insights/deloitte-review/issue-16/employee-engagement-strategies.html.

Berger-de Leon, Markus, Karel Dörner, Max Flötotto, and Tobias Henz. *Entrepreneurship Zeitgeist 2030*. New York: McKinsey & Company, 2021 https://www.mckinsey.com/industries/technology-media-and-telecommunications/our-insights/entrepreneurship-zeitgeist-2030.

Boyd, Milo. "World War 3 Fears Grow as Russian-Ukraine Crisis Could Escalate Global Conflict." *Daily Record*, February 24, 2022. https://www.dailyrecord.co.uk/news/uk-world-news/world-war-3-fears-grow-26324803.

Ferreira, Francisco H. G. "Inequality in the Time of COVID-19." *International Monetary Fund Finance & Development*, June 2021, https://www.imf.org/external/pubs/ft/fandd/2021/06/pdf/inequality-and-covid-19-ferreira.pdf.

Fires, Forests and the Future: A Crisis Raging Out of Control? Gland, Switzerland: World Wildlife Fund, 2020. https://wwfeu.awsassets.panda.org/downloads/wwf_fires_forests_and_the_future_report.pdf.

Goodreads. Quote by Albert Einstein: "*In the midst of every crisis, lies great opport....*" Accessed February 15, 2022. https://www.goodreads.com/quotes/10196552-in-the-midst-of-every-crisis-lies-great-opportunity.

Hughes, Jonathan, and Jeff Weiss. "Simple Rules for Making Alliances Work." *Harvard Business Review,* November 2007. https://hbr.org/2007/11/simple-rules-for-making-alliances-work.

Malnight, Thomas W., Ivy Buche, and Charles Dhanaraj. "Put Purpose at the Core of Your Strategy." *Harvard Business Review*, September–October 2019. https://hbr.org/2019/09/put-purpose-at-the-core-of-your-strategy.

Morgan, Jacob. "The Evolution of the Employee." *Jacob Morgan Inc.* September 16, 2014. https://thefutureorganization.com/evolution-employee.

Satell, Greg. *Cascades: How to Create a Movement That Drives Transformational Change.* New York: McGraw Hill, 2019.

Schwab, Klaus. "Now Is the Time for a 'Great Reset.'" *World Economic Forum*. Last modified June 3, 2020. https://www.weforum.org/agenda/2020/06/now-is-the-time-for-a-great-reset/.

Sinek, Simon (@Simon Sinek). "100 percent of employees are people. 100 percent of customers are people. 100 percent of investors are people. If you don't understand people, you don't understand business." LinkedIn, February 15, 2022. https://www.linkedin.com/posts/simonsinek_100-of-employees-are-people-100-of-customers-activity-6899197315018801153-sC2B.

The Deloitte Millennial Survey – Executive Summary. London: Deloitte Touche Tohmatsu Limited, 2014. https://www2.deloitte.com/content/dam/Deloitte/global/Documents/About-Deloitte/gx-dttl-2014-millennial-survey-report.pdf

World Economic Forum. "What Is the Great Reset? | Davos Agenda 2021." January 25, 2021. Video, 4:31. https://youtu.be/uPYx12x-JFUQ.

www.ingramcontent.com/pod-product-compliance
Lightning Source LLC
Chambersburg PA
CBHW070509160726
48003CB00004B/1489